Cycling THE ISLANDS

A Guide to Scenic Routes on
the San Juan and Gulf Islands

JOHN CROUCH

RMB

RMB | Rocky Mountain Books Ltd.
rmbooks.com
@rmbooks
facebook.com/rmbooks

Cataloguing data available from Library and Archives Canada
ISBN 978-1-77160-161-0 (pbk.)
Also available in electronic formats

Printed and bound in China by 1010 Printing International Ltd.

Distributed in Canada by Heritage Group Distribution and in the U.S. by Publishers Group West

For information on purchasing bulk quantities of this book, or to obtain media excerpts or invite the author to speak at an event, please visit rmbooks.com and select the "Contact Us" tab.

RMB | Rocky Mountain Books is dedicated to the environment and committed to reducing the destruction of old-growth forests. Our books are produced with respect for the future and consideration for the past.

We acknowledge the financial support of the Government of Canada through the Canada Book Fund and the Canada Council for the Arts, and of the province of British Columbia through the British Columbia Arts Council and the Book Publishing Tax Credit.

Disclaimer

The actions described in this book may be considered inherently dangerous activities. Individuals undertake these activities at their own risk. The information put forth in this guide has been collected from a variety of sources and is not guaranteed to be completely accurate or reliable. Many conditions and some information may change owing to weather and numerous other factors beyond the control of the authors and publishers. Individuals or groups must determine the risks, use their own judgment, and take full responsibility for their actions. Do not depend on any information found in this book for your own personal safety. Your safety depends on your own good judgment based on your skills, education, and experience.

It is up to the users of this guidebook to acquire the necessary skills for safe experiences and to exercise caution in potentially hazardous areas. The authors and publishers of this guide accept no responsibility for your actions or the results that occur from another's actions, choices, or judgments. If you have any doubt as to your safety or your ability to attempt anything described in this guidebook, do not attempt it.

Contents

GULF ISLANDS   89

The Routes

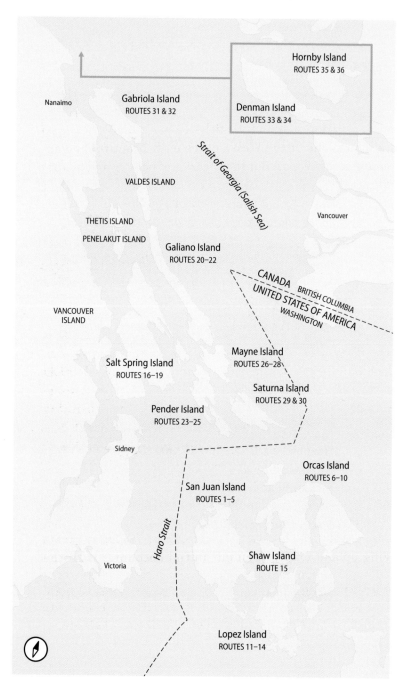

Hornby Island
ROUTES 35 & 36

Nanaimo

Gabriola Island
ROUTES 31 & 32

Denman Island
ROUTES 33 & 34

Strait of Georgia (Salish Sea)

VALDES ISLAND

Vancouver

THETIS ISLAND

PENELAKUT ISLAND

Galiano Island
ROUTES 20–22

CANADA BRITISH COLUMBIA
UNITED STATES OF AMERICA
WASHINGTON

VANCOUVER
ISLAND

Mayne Island
ROUTES 26–28

Salt Spring Island
ROUTES 16–19

Saturna Island
ROUTES 29 & 30

Pender Island
ROUTES 23–25

Sidney

Orcas Island
ROUTES 6–10

San Juan Island
ROUTES 1–5

Haro Strait

Shaw Island
ROUTE 15

Victoria

Lopez Island
ROUTES 11–14

Introduction

The string of islands cradled in the southern waters of the Salish Sea off the coast of British Columbia and Washington State form one of the West Coast's most beautiful and appealing archipelagos. But the vagaries of politics and history divided this homogeneous island cluster into two separate groups – the American San Juan Islands and the Canadian Gulf Islands – a story we'll get to.

The San Juans comprise four main islands, the largest of which is San Juan Island itself. Orcas Island is the next in size, with Lopez Island third. Shaw Island is by far the smallest of the group.

The Gulf Islands are the bigger of the two groups, consisting of eight islands. Like the San Juans, the group is known for those islands that are serviced by a ferry system. The largest of the Gulf Islands is Salt Spring Island. Gabriola Island, though less than half Salt Spring's size, is the second largest. Galiano Island is third with the remaining five – Pender, Saturna, Mayne, Denman and Hornby (the latter two the most northerly of this group* – being of similar but smaller size.

With the partial exception of Lopez, Shaw and Gabriola islands, the topography of all the islands is uniformly hilly. When we're on our bikes, the fact of ferry terminals being at sea level and all but the most fortunate of island residents living upland makes even our initial encounter with the

---

* The Gulf Islands are often dichotomized and referred to as the southern Gulf Islands and the northern Gulf Islands. This guidebook relates to the southern group but includes two of the northern group: Denman and Hornby islands.

islands a physical effort. "That #$%@ ferry hill" is the derisive expression heard on all the islands.

But how come two sets of islands? Here's how it happened.

Back in 1859 it was a silly matter of a pig being in the wrong place that plunged the ownership of the San Juan Islands into doubt – were they British (Canada was but a colony then) or part of the United States? The story goes that in the summer of that year, an American settler on San Juan Island shot dead a boar belonging to a Brit because the beast had invaded his garden. This incident was the final straw in a simmering territorial dispute between the British and the Americans. Both had troops on the island and both claimed sovereignty over it. Although the garden standoff ended peacefully, it took 13 years (1859–72) before an arbiter, Kaiser Wilhelm I of Germany, settled affairs by deciding that San Juan and its surrounding islands were indeed part of the United States of America.

This fact of geopolitics – and the rather tortuous zigzag boundary line that now delineates the Canada–US border, slicing through this large group of islands – does not detract from the islands' allure and attraction for anyone who sets eyes on them. The islands' craggy shorelines, protective bays, rising headlands and interior heights and valleys, and their mild, Mediterranean-type climate, are all strong enticements for us to go, with our bikes, and discover, explore and savour a land-scape and a way of life that are the envy of many an urbanite.

Not that the islands don't have settlements. They do. "Rural enclaves" is how one islander described them. But for the most part, the islands are lightly populated. The largest settlement is Friday Harbor on San Juan Island. It has a compact town centre and its own coffee bean roasting company and brew pub. So, too, does Salt Spring Island's Ganges, the largest community on the Gulf Islands. In fact, all the islands are peopled with enterprising folk who have optimized their artisanal skills and predilections to make each island an interesting and stimulating artistic and cultural environment.

As Edward Abbey, one of America's most respected naturalists, wrote in *Desert Solitaire*, "A man on foot, on horseback or on a bicycle will see more, enjoy more in one mile than the motorized tourist can in a hundred miles." And that's just one reason to explore the bucolic, peaceful and extraordinary variety of places and people that define the islands.

If you want to feel the sun on your arms and your legs, hear birdsong and smell the pungent aromas of saltwater, forest and open fields, take Abbey's words to heart. Jump on your bike and experience the beauty of the islands.

Getting to the Islands

Unless you're flying, have your own boat or are hiring a water taxi, the only way to the islands is by ferry. Here's what you need to know.

Ferries

There are two ferry systems that service the two groups of islands: Washington State Ferries for the San Juan Islands and BC Ferries for the Gulf Islands.

The San Juan Islands

Washington State Ferries uses Anacortes as its eastern gateway to the San Juans and Sidney, just north of Victoria in British Columbia, as its western terminal. The state ferries also provide an inter-island service between all the islands.

Information on schedules and fares is found at: www.wsdot.wa.gov/ferries.

The Gulf Islands

BC Ferries' main terminal for all the Gulf Islands is Swartz Bay, 32 km (20 mi) north of Victoria. Service from BC's

mainland to the islands is through BC Ferries' Tsawwassen terminal, 38 km (24 mi) south of Vancouver. Salt Spring Island has three BC Ferries terminals – Fulford Harbour for vessels from Swartz Bay, Long Harbour for vessels from Tsawwassen and other Gulf Islands, and Vesuvius Bay for vessels from Crofton on Vancouver Island. BC Ferries services Gabriola Island from Nanaimo Harbour and Denman and Hornby islands from Buckley Bay, 86 km (53 mi) north of Nanaimo.

Information on schedules and fares is found at: www.bcferries.com.

Accommodation

For a successful tour, planning is essential, and no aspect is more important than your accommodation. Whether you're proposing to stay at hotels, motels, lodges, B & Bs, hostels, guesthouses, cabins, or simply camping, making reservations is a good idea and can save you much heartache.

For each island represented in this book, on its first page, under information, I've provided one or two websites that I hope will assist you in planning your visit. They offer a list of accommodations, sights to see, things to do and contacts.

There's usually a wide range of accommodations on most of the islands. The exceptions are Shaw Island in the San Juan Islands and Saturna and Denman islands in the Gulf Islands. This is not to imply there are none but to suggest that, if you want to spend more than a day on each, you need to plan ahead. On Shaw Island, for instance, the only way to spend the night is in your own tent. And that might be a tenuous proposition, as there are only 11 campsites in Shaw Island County Park and they're on a first-come, first-served basis. For a look at the campsites go to: www.co.san-juan.wa.us/parks/camping.aspx.

On Saturna and Denman islands you have a bit more choice. Saturna has a few B & Bs, cottage rentals, a resort and

• *Boarding the ferry – Canadian style, Galiano Island.*

a lodge. Camping on the island is restricted to Narvaez Bay Day Use Area – part of the Gulf Islands National Park Reserve. There are only seven walk-in campsites on a first-come, first-served basis. To read more about these campsites go to www.parkscanada.gc.ca/gulfislands and follow the links: *Visitor Information, Facilities and Services*. Denman has limited accommodation, with a few B & Bs, guesthouses and cabins. The only camping on the island is at Fillongley Provincial Park. There are 10 reservable campsites available. The website is: www.env.gov.bc.ca/bcparks/.

In this book's individual island maps, campgrounds are indicated by the tent symbol.

Climate

One of the many draws to visiting the Gulf and San Juan islands is their climate. Both lie in a considerable rain shadow provided by the mountains of southern Vancouver Island and Washington's Olympic Peninsula. Climatologists characterize the islands as having a Mediterranean-type climate of mild winters with lots of moisture but little snow, and warm, relatively dry summers.

The Gulf Islands experience some of the highest sunshine hours in British Columbia and have the mildest climate in the whole of Canada. Temperatures for both island groups typically range from 0–23°C (32–73°F) over the course of a year, although summer temperatures are usually in the upper teens to low 20s (Celsius) (upper 60s to low 70s, Fahrenheit).

Annual precipitation totals can vary significantly across the islands but typically range anywhere from 64 to 102 cm (25 to 40 in), with most falling in the winter and July being the driest month. Optimum weather conditions for cycling the islands occur in June through September – the months that are the driest and warmest.

Flora and Fauna

The flora and fauna of the two island groups are almost identical. Coniferous trees, especially Douglas fir, are ubiquitous, with arbutus (madrone) and Garry oaks being well-represented, particularly on drier south- and southwest-facing slopes. Grassy balds (rocky outcrops) and grasslands are also common (Saturna and San Juan islands have large tracts of the latter).

Bald eagles are the defining bird species of the islands. Here, no other creature (except the orca whale) has such a presence and stature as this bird. They are everywhere – perched, watching, on the uppermost branches of the tallest trees; floating on thermals looking for a meal; swooping over sheltered water to clutch an unfortunate salmon from the shallows. And then there's the turkey vulture. For the bird lover, there is a profusion of birds on the islands – almost three hundred species call the islands their home or pay a visit.

No large predatory animals exist any longer on the islands. Bears were eliminated a century and a half ago by logging and hunting. Elk suffered the same fate. Because of the lack of predation, the black-tailed deer population is huge. Though cute to look at, they are becoming regarded as pests.

As you can imagine, there is an abundance of sea life in the surrounding ocean. Seals and sea lions are a common sight, as are river otters. Not too far offshore are orcas, humpback whales and, occasionally, grey whales. Often swimming ahead of inter-island ferry vessels are Dall's and Pacific white-sided porpoise.

How to Use this Book

All the route descriptions in this book follow a similar scheme. There is a short introduction intended to summarize what you're likely to see and experience while on the ride. Usually I write about the terrain and some aspect of the island you might find interesting. The introduction is also intended to whet your appetite for the ride rather than reveal every detail. The islands are for you to discover and explore. Too much information from me might interfere with that. (On the first page of each island section, I provide a brief summary of the island, including its size, population and one or two informational websites.)

Distance

Because the book describes routes in both Canada and the United States, measurements are calculated in each country's official measurement system. (The conversion is: 1 km = 0.6 mi; 1 mi = 1.6 km.)

Level

This, of course, indicates the level of difficulty of a route. For some riders, this is the most important piece of information in the whole book. Though not described in detail, the three designations – easy, moderate and strenuous – will, I hope, enable you to choose routes you can accomplish without too much discomfort. Remember, though, you're cycling on terrain that is inherently hilly, and "strenuous" is often written in the "level" description. Even though a route might be described as easy, it will inevitably have some variation in elevation along its course.

Highlights

These are places, buildings, roads, sites, parks, views, beaches I think might appeal to riders as they tour an island.

Start

This is the location of the route's start and, because most of the book's routes are loops, also its finish. I've assumed most cyclists will arrive on an island by ferry with their bikes and have, therefore, used the ferry terminal as the starting point for most of the routes.

The Route

I've used what I think is a simple and easy-to-comprehend format. First, there is the checkpoint number, for example: ④. Then follows the distance from the route's start in both kilometres and miles in parentheses: for example, (7.5 km/ 4.7 mi). This is followed by a written description of the route. The checkpoints correspond with those on the accompanying map. It's always a good idea to compare what you're reading with what you're seeing on the map. The directional right and left are rendered as "R" and "L" throughout.

Safe Cycling

The first principle of cycling on roads, in my mind, is to behave as if you belong there. And you do. But what does that mean? Well, it means riding according to the rules of the road (see below), riding confidently, with good bike-handling skills and giving clear hand signals; it means making eye contact with vehicle drivers, other cyclists and pedestrians at intersections and driveways. Belonging on the road means riding defensively, with awareness of what is going on around you, and riding conspicuously, i.e., wearing bright colours and reflective clothing.

According to British Columbia's Motor Vehicle Act (RSBC 1996, c. 318, Pt. 3) and Washington State Bicycle Laws, a cyclist has the same rights and duties as a driver of a motor vehicle. Following are some other requirements of the BC act as it pertains to cyclists.

A cyclist:
- must not ride on a sidewalk unless directed by official signage;
- must ride as near as practicable to the right side of the road except when turning left or overtaking;
- must not ride two abreast on the roadway;

- is not required to ride on any part of a road that is not paved;
- must use lights – white in front, red at the back – during hours of darkness;
- must have good brakes; and
- must wear a safety-approved helmet securely fastened and properly fitted.

Those wishing to read a more complete version of the act can do so at www.bikesense.bc.ca/bikesense-manual; read the chapter Cyclists and the Law.

Washington State cycling laws vary slightly from BC's. The two major exceptions are:

1. There is no statewide helmet requirement. It's left to individual counties to impose the requirement. The San Juan Islands are under the jurisdiction of San Juan County, which has no helmet law.
2. The state allows cyclists to ride two abreast.

For a more detailed reading of Washington State Bicycling Laws go to: www.wsdot.wa.gov/bike/Laws.

A ubiquitous road sign you'll find on both the island groups is the one depicting a cyclist and a car with the imperative "Share the Road." No matter what Washington State's law says about riding two abreast, the fact that many island roads have little or no shoulder means riding single file when you're with others makes complete sense. And much safer.

MAP LEGEND

Land

Park

Water

Inset

Route

Ferry route

Road

Border

Route direction

Start marker

Finish marker

Start/Finish marker

Route reference marker

Camping

Airport

Ferry terminal

Café / Restaurant

Landmark

Buck Bay, Olga Road, Orcas Island.

SAN JUAN ISLANDS

SAN JUAN ISLANDS

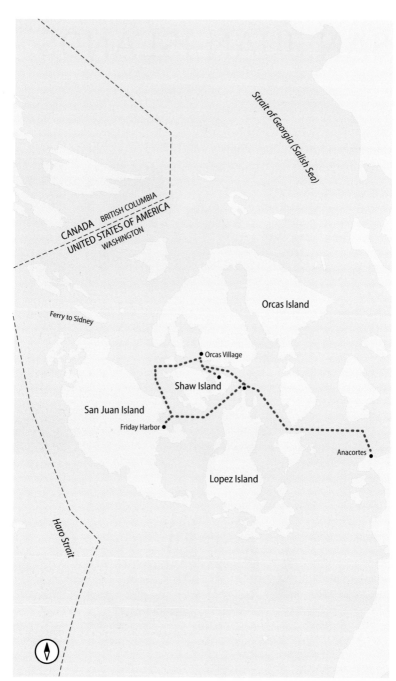

Introduction

The Pacific Northwest has been home to indigenous peoples for millennia. The Coast Salish First Nations used the San Juan Islands as a base from which to fish and harvest shellfish; they held gatherings on them and generally enjoyed themselves there. They knew a good place when they saw it, and their impeccable judgment continues to show us "moderns" where the beautiful places are today. In fact, the islands are often listed as being some of America's most desirable places to live.

Early white settlement of the islands didn't begin until the 1850s, when a trickle of British trappers and shepherds landed. Others were disillusioned American prospectors returning from BC's Cariboo and Fraser Canyon gold rushes. These folks arrived in the midst of the enmity between the British and the Americans over ownership of the islands. Once that was settled, the islands became calmer – but only just. Because of the islands' strategic location – slap between the shores of Washington State and British Columbia – they became useful to smugglers and rum-runners as places to conduct their illicit trades. Despite this "bad blood," the majority of settlers were honest, hard-working farmers, fishers and trades people.

But how to explain why three of the islands have Spanish names? Well, the region's early European explorers were predominantly British and Spanish. Both nations were colonizers and extraordinarily curious about the Pacific Coast, especially the waters of Puget Sound and the southern coast of British Columbia. Spanish explorer Francisco de Eliza, after charting the islands in the late 1700s, named both the group of islands and San Juan Island itself after his boss, the viceroy of Mexico, Juan Vicente de Güemes Padilla

Horcasitas y Aguayo, the second Count of Revillagigedo, affectionately known as "San Juan."

One of Eliza's officers – Gonzales López de Haro – was the first to clap eyes on the islands. He was honoured by having his name given to Lopez Island and to the body of water now known as Haro Strait.

Orcas Island's named derived – no, not from that magnificent creature the orca whale but from an abbreviated form of the viceroy of Mexico's name, Horcasitas.

The fourth and smallest of the group, Shaw Island, was named, unromantically, after an American naval officer.

British explorers did leave their mark in the region. The name Strait of Georgia was given by Captain George Vancouver for the British monarch King George III. Vancouver Island was named after George Vancouver.

The Routes

SAN JUAN ISLAND

SIZE: 142 km² (55 mi²)
POPULATION: 7,800
INFORMATION: www.visitsanjuans.com,
www.sanjuan.org

San Juan Island is the centrepiece of the island group. Though not the biggest by size, it has the largest population and is the administration hub for all the islands. The island township of Friday Harbor, with just over two thousand inhabitants, has a bustle that would rival a much larger place. The island's other harbour, Roche Harbor, has a much different feel. It has some of the daytime bustle and is dominated by the Hotel de Haro, a magnificent late-19th-century structure overlooking the harbour. It's part of a resort that includes a marina, restaurants and a store to complement its other amenities and accommodations. In 2009 the state declared the road between the two harbours, along with lengthy portions of other island roads, to be part of the state's Scenic Byway system. This designation means that the roads are well-maintained and a pleasure to ride on.

The island's largest park – San Juan National Historical Park – is in fact two separate pieces of land. The so-called "Pig War" saw to that. The north-island English Camp comprises one part of the park, while American Camp, several kilometres away on the island's southern tip, is the other. Lime Kiln Point State Park on the island's west shore is famous as an orca-watching vantage spot. In the spring, summer and fall, whale-watching boats from Victoria and Sidney, just across Haro Strait, flock to these shores, knowing there's a good chance of a sighting.

• *Camping at San Juan County Park, San Juan Island.*

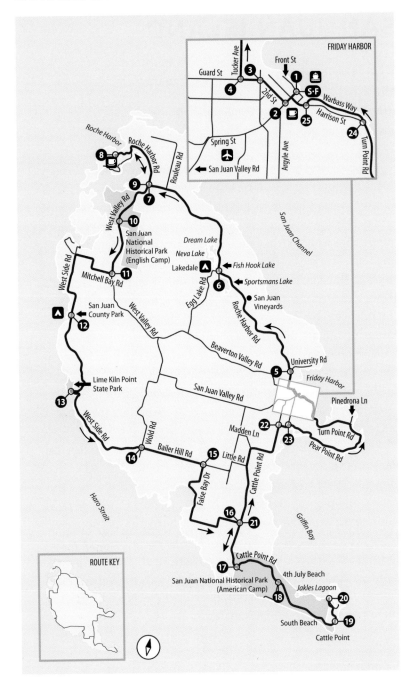

Tour of the Island

This is the longest ride in the book, but it's one of the most satisfying. You'll hit all of San Juan's main attractions and nip into a couple of its lesser-known nooks. Be prepared for some stunning ocean vistas, and make sure you're in good physical shape, have ample nutrition and your bike has enough gears for this roller-coaster of a ride. Along with Orcas Island's main roads, much of this San Juan Island route is part of Washington State's Scenic Byways system.

DISTANCE	81.5 km (50.3 mi)
LEVEL	Moderate to strenuous
HIGHLIGHTS	English Camp; American Camp; Roche Harbor; San Juan County Park; Lime Kiln Point State Park; False Bay; South Beach; Cattle Point Lighthouse
START	Ferry terminal in Friday Harbor

The Route

①   From the ferry terminal, turn R onto Front Street and then, at a small roundabout, turn L onto Spring Street.

② (0.2 km / 0.1 mi)   Turn R onto Second Street.

③ (0.5 km / 0.3 mi)   After passing the courthouse and theatre on your R, bear L and pass through the stop sign to continue on Guard Street.

④ (0.7 km / 0.4 mi)   Turn R at the next stop sign onto Tucker Avenue. (This is signed for Roche Harbor.)

⑤ (1.4 km / 0.9 mi)   Bear L as Tucker becomes Roche Harbor Road. (University Road bears R here.)

⑥ (7.5 km / 4.6 mi)   Egg Lake Road and Lakedale Resort are on your L.

⑦ (13.5 km / 8.3 mi)   Pass West Valley Road on your L. You'll return to this point after visiting Roche Harbor. After 2.0 km (1.2 mi), you'll pass under Roche Harbor Resort's archway. Keep to the paved, hilly road into the village centre.

⑧ (17.0 km / 10.5 mi)   Roche Harbor's village centre.

Retrace your ride to checkpoint 7.

⑨ (20.5 km / 12.7 mi)   Turn R onto West Valley Road.

⑩ (22.8 km / 14.1 mi)   Entrance to English Camp is on your R.

⑪ (25.3 km / 15.7 mi)   Turn R onto Mitchell Bay Road. After about 2.0 km (1.2 mi) at a sharp L bend, the road becomes West Side Road.

⑫ (30.4 km / 18.8 mi)   Entrance to San Juan County Park is on the R.

⑬ (34.5 km / 21.4 mi)   Stop sign. With the entrance to Lime Kiln Point State Park on the R, you turn L to continue on West Side Road.

⑭ (39.5 km / 24.5 mi)   West Side Road becomes Bailer Hill Road as Wold Road intersects from the L.

⑮ (42.5 km / 26.4 mi)   Turn R onto False Bay Drive. There is easy beach access to the bay 1.5 km (0.9 mi) along the road.

⑯ (48.0 km / 29.8 mi)   False Bay Drive reaches a junction with Cattle Point Road. Turn R onto Cattle Point Road.

⑰ (50.1 km / 31.1 mi)   Entrance to American Camp visitor centre on the R.

⑱ (51.9 km / 32.2 mi) Watch for entrances to: Fourth of July Beach and South Beach R, and Jakle's Lagoon L.

⑲ (55.6 km / 34.5 mi) Cattle Point's interpretive centre and lighthouse.

⑳ (57.2 km / 35.5 mi) End of the road at a small promontory and marina.

Retrace your ride to checkpoint 16.

㉑ (66.4 km / 41.2 mi) Continue past checkpoint 16 (False Bay Drive), keeping to Cattle Point Road.

㉒ (71.9 km / 44.6 mi) Turn R onto Argyle Avenue (opposite the airport landing strip).

㉓ (72.4 km / 44.9 mi) After a sweeping L bend, turn R onto Pear Point Road. This road becomes Turn Point Road at Pinedrona Lane on the R.

㉔ (79.8 km / 49.5 mi) At a one-way system, take the R fork onto Warbass Way and ride back into Friday Harbor.

㉕ (80.5 km / 50.0 mi) At the stop sign, turn R onto Harrison Street then R again onto East Street, riding the short distance to the ferry terminal.

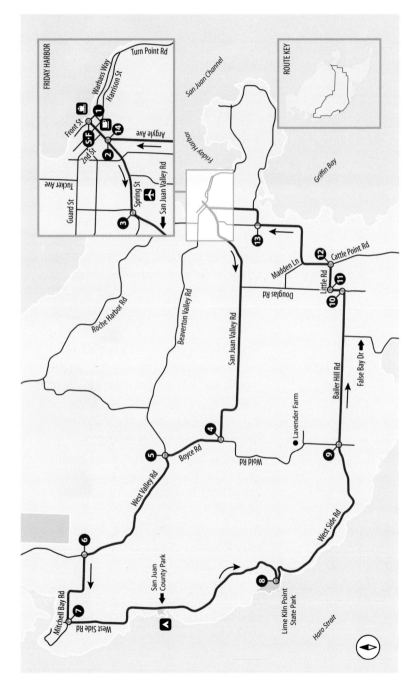

Mid Island Loop

Bisecting the island from east to west, this route goes from downtown Friday Harbor along two valley roads to the island's long and scenic west shore. There are two major hills on this ride – one down, one up. But, for the most part, the undulating roads make for a not-too-strenuous outing.

DISTANCE	37 km/23 mi
LEVEL	Moderate
HIGHLIGHTS	Central island farmland; San Juan County Park; Lime Kiln Point State Park and whale watching; views over Haro Strait to Victoria, British Columbia; lavender farm
START	Ferry terminal in Friday Harbor

The Route

①   From the ferry terminal, turn R onto Front Street and then turn L at its small roundabout onto Spring Street.

② (0.3 km / 0.1 mi)   Bear R as Spring Street climbs out of town. (Argyle Avenue is on the L.)

③ (1.2 km / 0.7 mi)   Spring Street becomes San Juan Valley Road on the edge of town.

④ (7.2 km / 4.4 mi)   Follow the road as it bears R to become Boyce Road. Wold Road goes L.

⑤ (8.8 km / 5.4 mi)   At an intersection, turn L onto West Valley Road. (Beaverton Valley Road goes R.)

⑥ (12.7 km / 7.8 mi)   Turn L onto Mitchell Bay Road.

⑦ (14.9 km / 9.2 mi)   At a second L turn, the road becomes West Side Road. (Snug Harbor Resort lies straight ahead.)

⑧ (20.0 km / 13.6 mi) Turn L at the stop sign. On the R is the entrance to Lime Kiln Point State Park.

⑨ (27.0 km / 17.7 mi) West Side Road becomes Bailer Hill Road. Wold Road is on the L. (A lavender farm is a short distance along Wold.)

⑩ (31.1 km / 19.3 mi) The road turns L to become Douglas Road.

⑪ (31.5 km / 19.5 mi) Turn R onto Little Road.

⑫ (32.2 km / 20.0 mi) Turn L onto Cattle Point Road. (To go R would take you to American Camp and Cattle Point.)

⑬ (35.2 km / 21.8 mi) Opposite the airport runway, turn R onto Argyle Avenue.

⑭ (36.9 km / 22.9 mi) Now in town, turn R at the stop sign onto Spring Street, and ride down to the ferry terminal.

• **Above:** *When do we get the paddles? San Juan County Park, San Juan Island.*

• **Right:** *Lighthouse, Lime Kiln Point State Park, San Juan Island, renowned for whale watching.*

American Camp and Cattle Point

This out-and-back route takes you to one of the most appealing parts of the island. Both aesthetically and historically, the island's southeastern tip is almost without parallel in the archipelago. The ride takes you through the length of American Camp National Historical Park and its grassy headlands. It's not a hard ride and is one that begs interruptions.

DISTANCE	33 km/20.5 mi (return)
LEVEL	Moderate
HIGHLIGHTS	American Camp Visitor Center; Fourth of July and South beaches; Jakle's Lagoon; Cattle Point lighthouse; Cape San Juan's promontory
START	Ferry terminal in Friday Harbor

The Route

①		From the ferry terminal, turn R onto Front Street and ride to the small roundabout, then turn L onto Spring Street.
②	(0.3 km / 0.1 mi)	At the top of the hill, turn L onto Argyle Avenue. (This is an awkward junction. Although you have the right-of-way, watch for oncoming traffic.)
③	(2.0 km / 1.2 mi)	Turn L onto Cattle Point Road.
④	(4.2 km / 2.6 mi)	Madden Lane goes R as you continue on Cattle Point Road.
⑤	(7.5 km / 4.6 mi)	False Bay Drive is on your R.
⑥	(9.6 km / 5.9 mi)	Entrance to American Camp Visitor Center on the R. Over the next kilometre, you pass the entrances to:

• *Cattle Point Lighthouse, San Juan Island.*

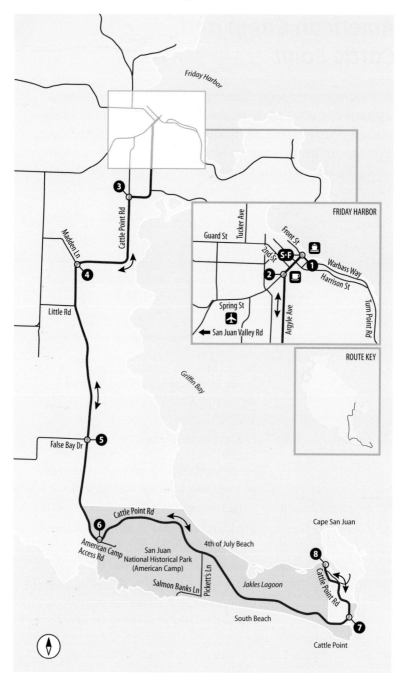

Friday Harbor

3 Cattle Point Rd

Madden Ln

4

Little Rd

FRIDAY HARBOR

Guard St

Tucker Ave

Front St

2nd St

S·F

1 Warbass Way

2

Harrison St

Spring St

Argyle Ave

Turn Point Rd

← San Juan Valley Rd

ROUTE KEY

Griffin Bay

False Bay Dr **5**

Cattle Point Rd

Cape San Juan

6

American Camp Access Rd

4th of July Beach

San Juan National Historical Park (American Camp)

Pickett's Ln

8

Cattle Point Rd

Salmon Banks Ln

Jakles Lagoon

South Beach

7

Cattle Point

Fourth of July Beach, South Beach R, and Jakle's Lagoon L.

⑦ (15.5 km / 9.6 mi) Cattle Point Interpretive Area is on the R.

⑧ (16.7 km / 10.3 mi) Enter Cape San Juan. There's a small promontory and marina at the end of the road. The rest of this enclave is private.

Retrace the route back to town.

• *Griffin Bay from Cape San Juan, San Juan Island.*

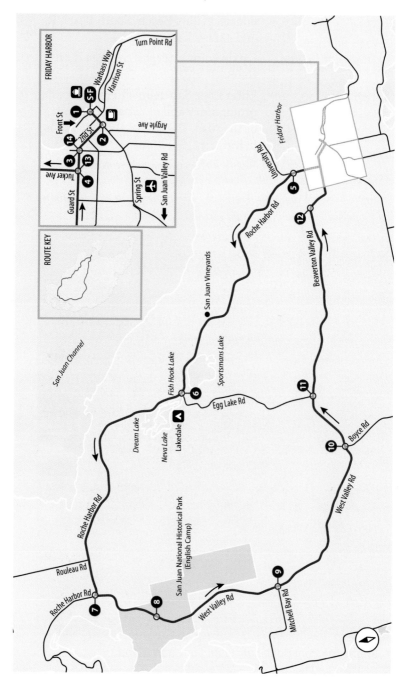

FRIDAY HARBOR

Turn Point Rd

Wanbass Way

Harrison St

S-F

Front St

Argyle Ave

2nd St

Tucker Ave

Guard St

Spring St

San Juan Valley Rd

ROUTE KEY

University Rd

Friday Harbor

Roche Harbor Rd

Beaverton Valley Rd

San Juan Vineyards

San Juan Channel

Sportsmans Lake

Fish Hook Lake

Egg Lake Rd

Dream Lake

Neva Lake

Lakedale

West Valley Rd

Boyce Rd

Roche Harbor Rd

San Juan National Historical Park
(English Camp)

Rouleau Rd

Roche Harbor Rd

West Valley Rd

Mitchell Bay Rd

North Island Loop

On the first part of this ride, you're exposed to some of the island's fertile farmland, including a picturesque vineyard. With a lake or two thrown in and the lush evergreen forest never far away, there's always an interesting or pleasant distraction from the rigours of riding as the route explores the northern interior of the island.

DISTANCE	30 km/18.6 mi
LEVEL	Moderate to strenuous
HIGHLIGHTS	English Camp National Historical Park; alpaca farm; island vineyard
START	Friday Harbor ferry terminal

The Route

① From the ferry terminal, turn R to ride along Front Street to a small roundabout, then turn L onto Spring Street.

② (0.2 km / 0.1 mi) Turn R onto Second Street.

③ (0.5 km / 0.3 mi) Bear L after a stop sign to continue on Guard Street.

④ (0.7 km / 0.4 mi) Turn R at the next stop sign onto Tucker Avenue.

⑤ (1.4 km / 0.8 mi) Bear L as Tucker becomes Roche Harbor Road. (Watch for the San Juan Vineyards a few kilometres farther along on your R.)

⑥ (7.5 km / 4.6 mi) Egg Lake Road and Lakedale Resort are on the L.

⑦ (13.5 km / 8.3 mi) At a R bend, turn L onto West Valley Road.

⑧ (15.7 km / 9.7 mi) Entrance to English Camp R. (You'll

pass an alpaca farm a short way farther along, also R.)

⑨ (18.2 km / 11.3 mi) Pass Mitchell Bay Road R. Continue on West Valley Road.

⑩ (22.1 km / 13.7 mi) At Boyce Road (on the R), West Valley Road becomes Beaverton Valley Road.

⑪ (23.5 km / 14.6 mi) Pass Egg Lake Road on your L.

⑫ (27.9 km / 17.3 mi) Beaverton Valley Road becomes Guard Street on the edge of town.

⑬ (28.9 km / 17.9 mi) Stop sign. Tucker Avenue goes L. Continue at the next stop sign onto Second Street.

⑭ (29.4 km / 18.2 mi) Turn L onto Spring Street, and ride the short distance down to Front Street and the ferry terminal.

- **Above:** *Alpaca farm on West Valley Road.*
- **Right:** *Wine tasting at San Juan Vineyards.*

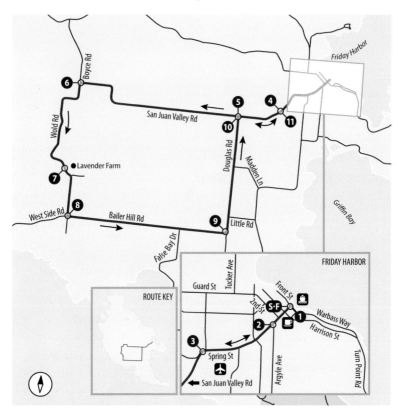

• *Lavender farm.*

Lavender Farm – Bailer Hill Road

It doesn't get much easier on San Juan Island on a bike than this route. Apart from leaving town, the only major climb is the gradual ride up Bailer Hill Road, and that's after the lavender farm.

DISTANCE	21 km/13 mi
LEVEL	Easy to moderate
HIGHLIGHTS	Lavender farm; farmland of San Juan Valley and Bailer Hill roads
START	Ferry terminal in Friday Harbor

The Route

①		From the ferry terminal, turn R onto Front Street and then L onto Spring Street at the small roundabout.
②	(0.3 km / 0.1 mi)	At the top of the hill, bear R to continue on Spring Street as you leave town. (Argyle Avenue goes L.)
③	(1.2 km / 0.7 mi)	After Spring Street arcs L, it becomes San Juan Valley Road.
④	(1.5 km / 0.9 mi)	Entrance to the airport is on the L.
⑤	(2.7 km / 1.6 mi)	Pass Douglas Road on the L.
⑥	(7.2 km / 4.4 mi)	Turn L onto Wold Road. Boyce Road goes to the R.
⑦	(10.3 km / 6.4 mi)	Lavender farm is on the L.
⑧	(11.2 km / 6.9 mi)	At the next junction, turn L onto Bailer Hill Road.
⑨	(15.3 km / 9.5 mi)	At a long L bend, Bailer Hill Road becomes Douglas Road.
⑩	(18.1 km / 11.2 mi)	Turn R onto San Juan Valley Road.
⑪	(19.5 / 12.1 mi)	Pass the airport entrance on your R and follow the road back into Friday Harbor via Spring Street.

ORCAS ISLAND

SIZE: 148 km² (57 mi²)

POPULATION: 5,200

INFORMATION: www.visitsanjuans.com,
www.orcasislandchamber.com

Orcas Island is the largest, by area, of the four San Juans. It's also the most ruggedly hilly of the group and has the highest point in the whole archipelago, Mount Constitution – a 733.6-m (2,407-ft) peak with splendid views of Mount Baker – well worth the climb. The mountain is part of Moran State Park, which is the largest by far of the islands' parks. The park is named after Robert Moran, a wealthy Seattle shipbuilder who, in 1905, built Moran Mansion, which is now part of Rosario Resort. A stone's throw from the park, the resort's main attraction is the mansion, which is part museum, part restaurant and part lounge.

Eastsound (yes, that's how it's written) is the island's centre, with lots of amenities, one of which is a great bike shop: Wildlife Cycles. Every August the shop organizes the Wildlife 100 tour of the San Juan Islands. You get to ride all the islands for just $10.

There are a number of nooks and crannies on Orcas, and some of their names are intriguingly descriptive: Doe Bay, Deer Harbor, Obstruction Pass, Orcas Village. (I haven't discovered how Olga became a place name yet, but I have my suspicions.)

• *View from the top, Mt. Constitution.*

ORCAS ISLAND ROUTE 6

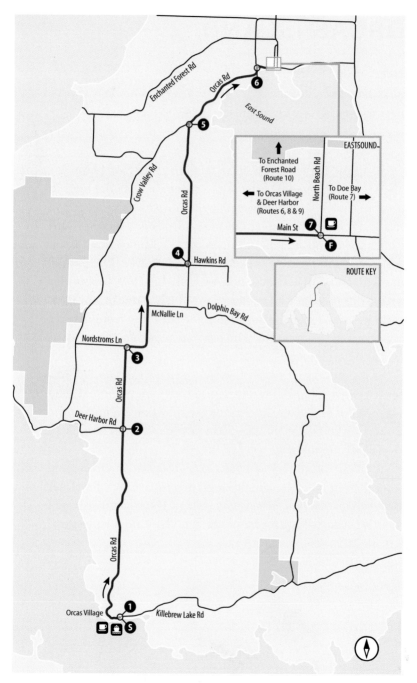

Orcas Village to Eastsound

This route is the most direct and quickest to the island centre of Eastsound. It's a little up and down, but, believe it or not, it's a relatively gentle introduction to the island's roads.

DISTANCE	14 km/9 mi
LEVEL	Moderate
HIGHLIGHTS	Orcas Village; Eastsound; island farmland
START	Orcas Village ferry terminal

The Route

①   Exit the ferry terminal and turn L.

② (4.2 km / 2.6 mi)   Pass Deer Harbor Road on your L. (This road leads to West Sound and Deer Harbor.)

③ (5.8 km / 3.6 mi)   Nordstroms Lane is on the L, connecting to Crow Valley Road.

④ (8.6 km / 5.3 mi)   Bear L at an information board at the junction of Dolphin Bay Road and Hawkins Road.

⑤ (11.4 km / 7.1 mi)   Bear R at the junction of Crow Valley Road (on the L).

⑥ (13.3 km / 8.2 mi)   Turn R onto Main Street in the town of Eastsound.

⑦ (13.7 km / 8.4 mi)   Turn L at the three-way stop sign onto North Beach Road. You're now in the heart of Eastsound.

Camping on Cascade Lake, Orcas Island.

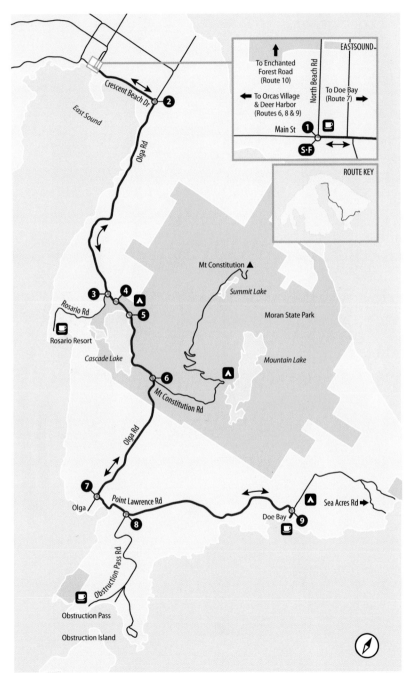

EASTSOUND

To Enchanted
Forest Road
(Route 10)

← To Orcas Village
& Deer Harbor
(Routes 6, 8 & 9)

North Beach Rd

To Doe Bay
(Route 7) →

Main St **1**

S·F

ROUTE KEY

Crescent Beach Dr.

2

East Sound

Olga Rd

Mt Constitution ▲

Summit Lake

Moran State Park

3 **4**

5

Rosario Rd

Rosario Resort

Cascade Lake

Mountain Lake

6

Mt Constitution Rd

Olga Rd

7

Olga

Point Lawrence Rd

Doe Bay **9**

Sea Acres Rd →

8

Obstruction Pass Rd

Obstruction Pass

Obstruction Island

Eastsound to Doe Bay

This is one of the most demanding roads on the San Juans – but it's worth it. For the most part the road has a usable shoulder, and its two tight bends are easily negotiated. The reward, of course, is Doe Bay. The sheltered bay, general store, resort cottages and secluded campsites, not to mention the scrumptious food served at its café, are all welcome sights. The catch is – you've guessed it – you must make the return journey.

DISTANCE	35 km/22 mi (Return to Eastsound)
LEVEL	Moderate to strenuous
HIGHLIGHTS	Rosario Resort and Moran Mansion; Moran State Park and Cascade Lake; Mount Constitution; Olga Village; Obstruction Point; Doe Bay Resort
START	Corner of North Beach Road and Main Street, Eastsound

The Route

① Ride east along | Main Street, which soon becomes Crescent Beach Drive.

② (1.8 km / 1.1 mi) | Turn R onto Olga Road.

③ (6.8 km / 4.2 mi) | On the R is the entrance road to Rosario Resort and Moran Mansion Museum (2.0 km / 1.2 mi away, down a steep hill).

④ (7.0 km / 4.3 mi) | Pass under the archway of Moran State Park. (The entrance to the park's registration booth is a short distance up on the R.)

⑤ (7.7 km / 4.7 mi) | The park's day-use area on Cascade Lake is on your R.

⑥ (9.1 km / 5.6 mi) | Mount Constitution is on your L. At 739 m (2,424 ft), its summit is the highest point on the San Juan and

Gulf islands. The 8.0-km (5.0-mi) road to the top has an average grade of 8 per cent – a good workout if you take it!

(7) (12.4 km / 7.7 mi) The road makes an abrupt L turn onto Point Lawrence Road. To go straight leads to a dead end at the village of Olga 0.5 km (0.3 mi) away. Olga has a post office and (sometimes) a small store.

(8) (13.3 km / 8.2 mi) Pass Obstruction Pass Road on your R. (Obstruction Pass State Park is 1.5 km [0.9 mi] on the R along this road, and the Lieber Haven Resort and Marina is at the end of the road – a further 1.5 km [0.9 mi].)

(9) (17.8 km / 11.0 mi) Entrance to Doe Bay Resort is on your R. (If you wish to ride farther along Point Lawrence Road, you can do so for another 3.0 km [1.8 mi] and then turn around at the end of Sea Acres Road.)

Retrace your ride back to Eastsound.

• *Moran Mansion, Rosario Resort.*

Eastsound to Deer Harbor

Crow Valley Road is one of those delightful pastoral roads that you're happy just to be riding on. It has no major hills and few bends, and it runs by hedgerow, forest and hills in almost equal measure. As well, it's only a short distance from the ride's start. Deer Harbor is essentially a resort and marina. The road past it to Pole Pass is very quiet, with one attractive clifftop lookout. If you agree with me about Crow Valley Road, forget my directions back via Orcas Road and take Crow Valley instead.

DISTANCE	40 km/25 mi (Return to Eastsound)
LEVEL	Moderate
HIGHLIGHTS	Crow Valley Road; Turtleback Mountain trailhead; West Sound Café; Deer Harbor, Pole Pass lookout
START	Corner of North Beach Road and Main Street, Eastsound

The Route

①		Ride west along Main Street in the direction of Orcas Road.
②	(0.3 km / 0.2 mi)	Turn L onto Orcas Road.
③	(2.2 km / 1.4 mi)	At a Y in the road, bear R to take Crow Valley Road. Orcas Road goes L.
④	(3.3 km / 2.0 mi)	Stop sign. Continue straight on Crow Valley Road. West Beach Road goes R. (At 4.8 km [3.0 mi] on your R is the trailhead to Turtleback Mountain.)
⑤	(7.6 km / 4.7 mi)	Stop sign. Continue straight. The road L is Nordstroms Lane – a connector to Orcas Road.
⑥	(9.1 km / 5.6 mi)	Turn R at this junction onto Deer Harbor Road. West Sound Café is here. To the L is the small community of West Sound.

ORCAS ISLAND ROUTE 8

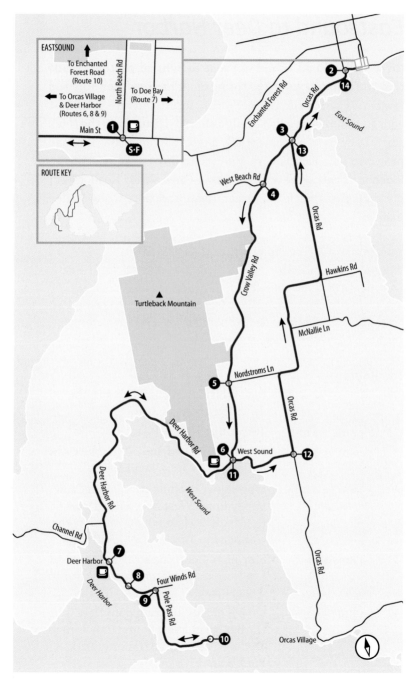

EASTSOUND

To Enchanted Forest Road (Route 10)

To Orcas Village & Deer Harbor (Routes 6, 8 & 9)

North Beach Rd

To Doe Bay (Route 7)

Main St ❶

S·F

ROUTE KEY

❷
⓮
East Sound

Enchanted Forest Rd

Orcas Rd

❸
⓭

West Beach Rd
❹

Orcas Rd

Hawkins Rd

Crow Valley Rd

Turtleback Mountain

McNallie Ln

Nordstroms Ln
❺

Orcas Rd

Deer Harbor Rd

West Sound
❻
⓬

Deer Harbor Rd
⓫

West Sound

Channel Rd

Orcas Rd

Deer Harbor ❼
❽
Four Winds Rd

Deer Harbor
❾
Pole Pass Rd

⓾

Orcas Village

⑦ (15.8 km / 9.8 mi)   The entrance to Deer Harbor Marina is on your R. A café and small store are here.

⑧ (16.3 km / 10.1 mi)   On the R you'll find a rideable 0.5-km (0.3-mi) public path that includes a clifftop lookout. It starts opposite Bear Cove Lane and ends at Windward Lane.

⑨ (17.3 km / 10.7 mi)   At Four Winds Road, bear R as Deer Harbor Road becomes Pole Pass Road.

⑩ (19.0 km / 11.8 mi)   The road comes to a dead end here. Retrace the route to checkpoint 6.

⑪ (29.0 km / 18.0 mi)   At this junction, continue straight on Deer Harbor Road to ride through West Sound.

⑫ (30.4 km / 18.8 mi)   Turn L onto Orcas Road.

⑬ (37.7 km / 23.4 mi)   Pass Crow Valley Road junction on your L.

⑭ (39.5 km / 24.5 mi)   Turn R onto Main Street and ride back into Eastsound.

- *Choose your ride. Bike store, Eastsound, Orcas Island.*

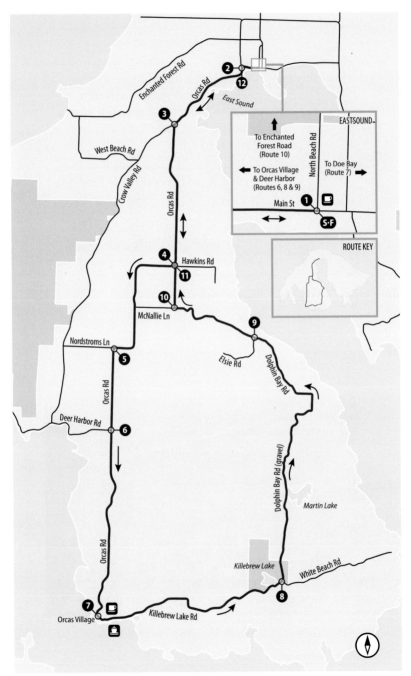

Enchanted Forest Rd

Orcas Rd

East Sound

2
12

3

West Beach Rd

Crow Valley Rd

Orcas Rd

EASTSOUND

To Enchanted
Forest Road
(Route 10)

To Orcas Village
& Deer Harbor
(Routes 6, 8 & 9)

North Beach Rd

To Doe Bay
(Route 7)

Main St   **1**

ROUTE KEY

4 Hawkins Rd
11

10
McNallie Ln

Nordstroms Ln

5

9

Elsie Rd

Dolphin Bay Rd

Orcas Rd

Deer Harbor Rd   **6**

Dolphin Bay Rd (gravel)

Martin Lake

Orcas Rd

Killebrew Lake

White Beach Rd

8

7
Orcas Village   Killebrew Lake Rd

Eastsound–Killebrew Lake Loop

Make sure you choose dry weather for this excursion onto a gravel road, otherwise you could get rather mucky. Thankfully, the dirt portion of this squarish loop is only about 6 km (3.7 mi) long and starts just past Killebrew Lake (pronounced KILL-A-BREW) – a great place to cool off on a hot day. This part of Orcas is lightly populated, and Dolphin Bay Road travels mostly through forested terrain – thus the gravel section. If you enjoy the quiet that forested roads can bring, this loop is perfect.

DISTANCE	31.5 km/19.6 mi
LEVEL	Moderate (some gravel)
HIGHLIGHTS	Orcas Village; Killebrew Lake; forested Dolphin Bay Road
START	Corner of North Beach Road and Main Street, Eastsound

The Route

①   Ride west along Main Street toward Orcas Road.

② (0.3 km / 0.2 mi)   Turn L onto Orcas Road.

③ (2.2 km / 1.3 mi)   Pass Crow Valley Road on the R.

④ (5.0 km / 3.1 mi)   Road bears R at Dolphin Bay Road junction.

⑤ (7.8 km / 4.8 mi)   Nordstroms Lane, R, leads to Crow Valley Road.

⑥ (9.4 km / 5.8 mi)   Deer Harbor Road, R, leads to West Sound and Deer Harbor.

⑦ (13.6 km / 8.4 mi)   Orcas Village. Continue past the ferry terminal onto Killebrew Lake Road.

⑧ (17.4 km / 10.8 mi)   Killebrew Lake is on your L. A little farther, as the road curves L,

Killebrew Lake Road becomes Dolphin Bay Road. (Gravel road surface begins.)

⑨ (23.6 km / 14.6 mi) Elsie Road on your L marks the resumption of pavement.

⑩ (25.5 km / 15.8 mi) Turn R at the McNallie Lane junction onto a continuation of Dolphin Bay Road.

⑪ (26.4 km / 16.4 mi) At the junction of Dolphin Bay Road, Orcas Road and Hawkins Road, continue straight onto Orcas Road.

⑫ (31.1 km / 19.3 mi) Turn R onto Eastsound's Main Street and ride the short distance to the route's start.

• **Above:** *Overlooking Indian Island and East Sound from Eastsound Park.* • **Right:** *Artwork, Eastsound, Orcas Island.*

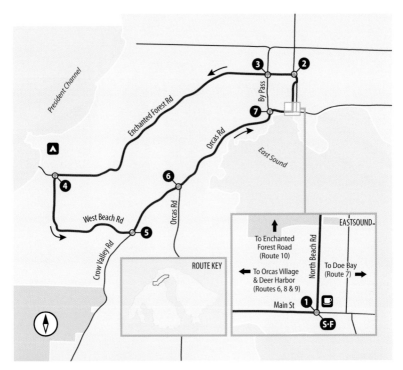

• *Eastsound hostel, Orcas Island.*

Eastsound – Enchanted Forest Road Loop

One can hardly be blamed for checking out a road when it's called Enchanted Forest. But is it enchanted? The locals won't say. Admitted, it is a forested road with tall fir and cedars on either side, ferns providing rich and abundant undergrowth. And it is a delight to ride along, especially on a hot summer's day and you're searching for shade. So, on that scorching afternoon when you feel like a short spin, think Enchanted Forest Road. (Perhaps it is enchanted after all.)

DISTANCE	10 km/6.2 mi
LEVEL	Moderate
HIGHLIGHTS	Delightful forest road; West Beach Resort
START	Orcas Island Chamber of Commerce, 65 North Beach Road, Eastsound

The Route

① | With the Chamber of Commerce building on your L, ride up North Beach Road to its junction with School Road and Prune Alley. Turn L onto a continuation of North Beach Road.

② (0.5 km / 0.3 mi) | Turn L almost immediately onto Enchanted Forest Road.

③ (1.0 km / 0.6 mi) | Cross Lover's Lane (aka the bypass road).

④ (5.0 km / 3.1 mi) | Swing L onto West Beach Road. (The entrance to West Beach Resort is straight ahead.)

⑤ (7.1 km / 4.4 mi) | Turn L onto Crow Valley Road at this three-way-stop sign.

⑥ (8.2 km / 5.1 mi) | At the stop sign, cross and turn L onto Orcas Road.

⑦ (10.0 km / 6.2 mi) | Turn R onto Main Street and ride into Eastsound and to the route's start.

LOPEZ ISLAND

SIZE: 77 km² (30 mi²)
POPULATION: 2,400
INFORMATION: www.visitsanjuans.com, www.lopezisland.com

Sometimes called the "relaxed" island, Lopez Island is, in a number of ways, the antithesis of its two larger sister islands. In contrast to San Juan and Orcas, Lopez is much flatter, more rural, has fewer amenities and a population that is roughly the size of Friday Harbor's. From a cyclist's perspective, once you've climbed the ferry hill, Lopez Island is a rider's paradise. With long, relatively flat and straight roads and corners that are often as easygoing as the islanders' lifestyle, riders can relax and enjoy the ride.

Lopez Village reflects the laid-back atmosphere of the whole island. Small but spacious and uncluttered, it's the opposite of Friday Harbor and Eastsound. The island's parks are not large either. Odlin County Park and Spencer Spit State Park are ideal for camping, picnicking, beachcombing and birding. They have no trails to speak of. Shark Reef Sanctuary, on the island's west side, has a rocky shoreline, and when the mists are not swirling, you can see seals and take in views of islets and the southern beaches of San Juan Island. Iceberg Point in Agate Beach County Park and Watmough Head's Point Colville have the island's two most rewarding hikes. But what the island really has to offer is its bucolic flavour – open fields dotted with grazing sheep or cattle are everywhere, as are wheat crops swaying in the summer winds and roads that seem to take their time taking you anywhere.

• *Picnic at Outer Bay, Agate Beach County Park, Lopez Island.*

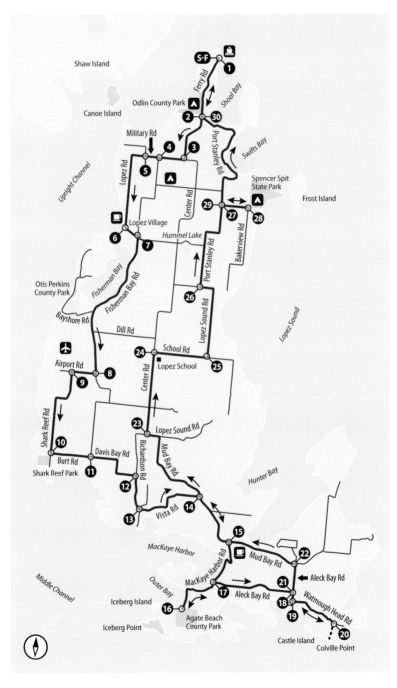

Tour of the Island

This long loop makes for a gorgeous day's outing. Not only are the roads in good condition with little traffic, the traffic itself is hospitable. And it's a relatively easy island to cycle – apart from the ferry hill, there are no major hills to speak of. The view from the saddle on this ride conveys a sense of spaciousness, with large swaths of land under cultivation. At almost every turn, there's something to arrest the eye. On the west side there's long, curving Fisherman Bay and Shark Reef Sanctuary. There's Iceberg Point in Agate Beach County Park at the island's south end. There's Spencer Spit State Park on the northeast corner. And there's much more in between. With a ride of this length and with so much to see and enjoy, do yourself a favour – give yourself lots of time.

DISTANCE	60 km/37 mi
LEVEL	Moderate
HIGHLIGHTS	Lopez Village; Fisherman Bay; Shark Reef Sanctuary; Agate Beach County Park; Point Colville; Spencer Spit State Park; Port Stanley
START	Lopez Island ferry terminal

The Route

①		Leave the ferry terminal and ride up the long hill.
②	(1.8 km / 1.1 mi)	Entrance to Odlin County Park on the R, Port Stanley Road on the L.
③	(3.3 km / 2.0 mi)	Bear R onto Fisherman Bay Road. Center Road goes L.
④	(4.1 km / 2.5 mi)	As the road curves L, turn R onto Military Road.
⑤	(4.5 km / 2.8 mi)	Military Road turns R. You continue straight onto what is now Lopez Road.

⑥ (7.1 km / 4.4 mi)   Bear L into Lopez Village, keeping to Lopez Road.

⑦ (7.5 km / 4.7 mi)   Ride through the village and turn R onto Fisherman Bay Road.

⑧ (12.2 km / 7.6 mi)   Turn R onto Airport Road. (Signed for the golf course.)

⑨ (13.0 km / 8.0 mi)   Turn L onto Shark Reef Road.

⑩ (15.7km / 9.7 mi)   Turn L onto Burt Road. (A short distance past Burt Road on the R is the entrance to Shark Reef Sanctuary, a national wildlife refuge.)

⑪ (17.0 km / 10.6 mi)   At the stop sign, continue straight onto Davis Bay Road.

⑫ (18.8 km / 11.7 mi)   Turn R at a stop-signed intersection onto Richardson Road.

⑬ (19.8 km / 12.3 mi)   At the junction of Paradise and Vista roads, bear L onto Vista Road. Richardson goes to the R.

⑭ (22.0 km / 13.7 mi)   Turn R at the next stop-signed junction, onto Mud Bay Road.

⑮ (23.7 km / 14.7 mi)   Just before the Southend General Store and Restaurant, turn R onto MacKaye Harbor Road.

⑯ (26.6 km / 16.5 mi)   You're now at Agate Beach County Park. (Iceberg Point is accessible by a walk-in trail at the end of the road.)

Retrace the route to arrive at the next checkpoint.

⑰ (28.6 km / 17.8 mi)   Turn R onto Aleck Bay Road.

⑱ (31.1 km / 19.3 mi)   As Aleck Bay Road turns abruptly L, you turn R onto Watmough Head Road – a portion of which is gravel – and continue on to the Point Colville trailhead. (If you choose not

---

• *Beach décor at Port Stanley, Lopez Island.*

to go to Point Colville, turn L here onto the continuation of Aleck Bay Road and ride to checkpoint 22.)

⑲ (32.6 km / 20.3 mi) Turn L at the road's junction with Huggins Road to continue on Watmough Head Road. As the gravel deteriorates, find a marked walk-in trail on your R to Point Colville – a high bluff area overlooking Castle Island.

⑳ (33.4 km / 20.7 mi) Retrace the route back to checkpoint 18.

㉑ (35.4 km / 22.0 mi) Continue north on Aleck Bay Road.

㉒ (36.2 km / 22.5 mi) At a four-way intersection, turn L onto Mud Bay Road. (You soon pass a general store on your L.)

㉓ (43.2 km / 26.8 mi) At Mud Bay Road's junction with Richardson and Center roads, sweep R onto Center Road.

㉔ (45.6 km / 28.3 mi) Immediately after the Lopez Island School on your R, turn R onto School Road.

㉕ (47.3 km / 29.4 mi) Bear L onto Lopez Sound Road, going north.

㉖ (49.7 km / 30.9 mi) Shortly after a sharp L bend, turn R at a stop sign onto Port Stanley Road.

㉗ (52.5 km / 32.6 mi) Turn R onto Bakerview Road leading to Spencer Spit State Park. (To avoid the park, continue on Port Stanley Road through Swifts Bay to checkpoint 30.)

㉘ (53.4 km / 33.2 mi) Park entrance.

Retrace the route to arrive at the next checkpoint.

• *Leaving Lopez, with Orcas Island in background.*

㉙ (54.3 km / 33.7 mi)   At Bakerview Road's junction with Port Stanley Road, turn R to ride toward the shore of Swifts Bay.

㉚ (58.4 km / 36.2 mi)   After riding along Swifts Bay then up a short climb, turn R onto Ferry Road and descend the hill back to the ferry terminal. (If you're heading back to Lopez Village, either follow checkpoints 3 through 6 or continue on Fisherman Bay Road at checkpoint 4 – a slightly quicker route.)

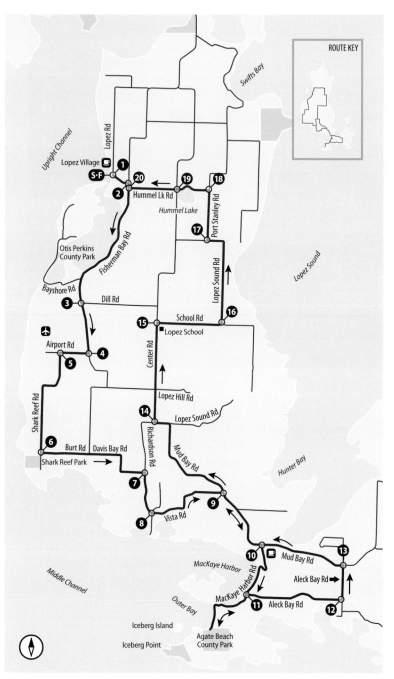

ROUTE KEY

Swifts Bay

Upright Channel

Lopez Rd

Lopez Village

1

S·F

2

20

Hummel Lk Rd

19

18

Port Stanley Rd

Hummel Lake

17

Otis Perkins
County Park

Fisherman Bay Rd

Lopez Sound Rd

Lopez Sound

Bayshore Rd

Dill Rd

3

School Rd

16

15

Lopez School

Airport Rd

4

5

Center Rd

Shark Reef Rd

Lopez Hill Rd

14

Lopez Sound Rd

6

Burt Rd   Davis Bay Rd

Richardson Rd

Mud Bay Rd

Hunter Bay

Shark Reef Park

7

Vista Rd

8

9

Middle Channel

MacKaye Harbor

10

Mud Bay Rd

13

MacKaye Harbor Rd

Aleck Bay Rd

Outer Bay

MacKaye Harbor Rd

11

Aleck Bay Rd

12

Iceberg Island

Iceberg Point

Agate Beach
County Park

South Island Loop

On this half-day loop ride you can take your time exploring the island's southern reaches. There's an interesting mix of "must visit" sights such as Shark Reef Sanctuary and Iceberg Point and of rural and shoreline Lopez as you follow the paved roads of this mostly easy route.

DISTANCE	41.5 km/25.8 mi
LEVEL	Easy to moderate
HIGHLIGHTS	Views over Fisherman Bay; Shark Reef Sanctuary; Agate Beach County Park; Hummel Lake
START	Lopez Village Park

The Route

①   From the park, turn L onto Lopez Road.

② (0.2 km / 0.1 mi)   At the end of the village, turn R onto Fisherman Bay Road.

③ (3.9 km / 2.4 mi)   Pass Dill Road, a major road to your L.

④ (4.7 km / 2.9 mi)   Turn R onto Airport Road. (Signed for the golf course.)

⑤ (5.5 km / 3.4 mi)   Turn L onto Shark Reef Road.

⑥ (8.2 km / 5.1 mi)   Turn L onto Burt Road. (A little way past Burt, on the R, is Shark Reef Sanctuary, a national wildlife refuge.) Continue straight as Burt joins and becomes Davis Bay Road.

⑦ (11.3 km / 7.0 mi)   At the stop-signed intersection, turn R onto Richardson Road.

⑧ (12.3 km / 7.6 mi)   As Richardson meets Paradise and Vista roads, bear slightly L to take Vista Road.

⑨ (14.5 km / 9.0 mi) Turn R at the next stop sign onto Mud Bay Road.

⑩ (16.2 km / 10.1 mi) Just before a store and restaurant, turn R onto MacKaye Harbor Road. Ride to the road's end at Agate Beach County Park. (The trail to Iceberg Point is here.)

Retrace the route to checkpoint 11.

⑪ (21.1 km / 13.1 mi) Turn R onto Aleck Bay Road.

⑫ (23.6 km / 14.7 mi) At a T junction, turn L onto a continuation of Aleck Bay Road.

⑬ (24.4km/15.2 mi) At the end of Aleck Bay Road, turn L onto Mud Bay Road.

⑭ (31.4 km / 19.5 mi) As Mud Bay Road meets Richardson and Center roads, sweep R onto Center Road.

⑮ (33.8 km / 21.0 mi) Turn R after Lopez Island School onto School Road.

⑯ (35.5 km / 22.1 mi) Bear sharply L as School Road becomes Lopez Sound Road.

⑰ (37.9 km / 23.6 mi) At the stop sign, turn R onto Port Stanley Road.

⑱ (39.1 km / 24.3 mi) As the forest becomes open fields, turn L onto Hummel Lake Road. Hummel Lake soon appears on the L.

⑲ (40.0 km / 24.9 mi) Cross Center Road to stay on Hummel. (Beach access to Hummel Lake is on your L at this intersection.)

⑳ (41.2 km / 25.6 mi) At the next stop sign, turn R onto Fisherman Bay Road and then take the first L onto Lopez Road to ride back to the village park.

• *Wheat fields, Lopez Island.*

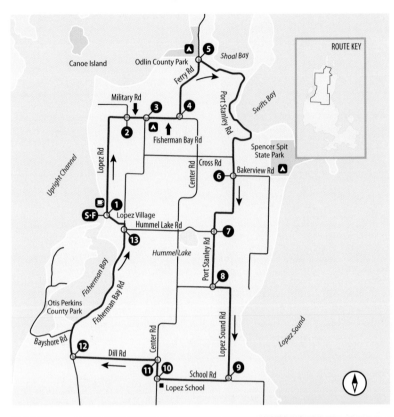

- *Primo campsite at Spencer Spit, Lopez Island.*

North Island Loop

This short route passes two of the island's biggest parks – Odlin County Park and Spencer Spit State Park. Besides having large campgrounds, both parks have sandy beaches and walk-in/bike-in picnic areas. You'll also ride along the sweeping, sandy shore of Port Stanley's Swifts Bay. Hummel Lake is at the centre of the island's northern half – and you'll pass close to that, too.

DISTANCE	22.5 km/14 mi
LEVEL	Easy to moderate
HIGHLIGHTS	Odlin County Park; Port Stanley's Swifts Bay; Spencer Spit State Park
START	Lopez Village Park

The Route

① From the park, turn R onto Lopez Road and ride north.

② (2.6 km / 1.6 mi) After a sharp R bend, Lopez Road becomes Military Road.

③ (3.0 km / 1.9 mi) At the stop sign, turn L onto Fisherman Bay Road.

④ (3.8 km / 2.4 mi) Follow Fisherman Bay Road as it bears L to become Ferry Road.

⑤ (5.3 km / 3.3 mi) Opposite the entrance to Odlin County Park, turn R onto Port Stanley Road.

⑥ (9.3 km / 5.8 mi) Pass Bakerview Road, L. (If you want to visit Spencer Spit State Park, the entrance is at the end of this road about 1 km [0.6 mi] away.)

⑦ (11.0 km / 6.8 mi) After two sweeping bends, pass Hummel Lake Road, R.

⑧ (12.1 km / 7.5 mi)   At the intersection, turn L onto Lopez Sound Road.

⑨ (14.5 km / 9.0 mi)   Follow the road as it sweeps R to become School Road.

⑩ (16.2 km / 10.0 mi)   Turn R onto Center Road, opposite Lopez Island School, L.

⑪ (16.6 km / 10.3 mi)   After passing a building supplies store, turn L onto Dill Road.

⑫ (18.7 km / 11.6 mi)   Bear R onto Fisherman Bay Road.

⑬ (22.4 km / 13.9 mi)   With the fire hall on your L, turn L onto Lopez Road to ride the short distance back to the village park.

• *Bikes galore.*

Mid Island Loop

This route explores the geographical heart of the island. The roads are primarily flat (there's one hill) and thread through a mixture of cultivated farmland, homesteads and forest. The route even passes the only lake on the island – Hummel Lake.

DISTANCE	14 km/8.7 mi
LEVEL	Easy to moderate
HIGHLIGHTS	Fisherman Bay; quiet country roads; Hummel Lake
START	Lopez Village Park

The Route

① From the park, turn L onto Lopez Road.

② (0.2 km / 0.1 mi) At the end of the village, turn R onto Fisherman Bay Road.

③ (3.9 km / 2.4 mi) Take Dill Road, the first major road to your L.

④ (5.8 km / 3.6 mi) Turn R onto Center Road.

⑤ (6.2 km / 3.8 mi) Opposite the hydro station, turn L onto School Road. (Lopez Island School is on the corner.)

⑥ (7.8 km / 4.8 mi) Bear sharply L as School Road becomes Lopez Sound Road.

⑦ (9.8 km / 6.1 mi) Lopez Sound Road turns abruptly L.

⑧ (10.3 km / 6.4 mi) At the stop sign, turn R onto Port Stanley Road.

⑨ (11.5 km / 7.1 mi) As the forest becomes open fields, turn L onto Hummel Lake Road. Hummel Lake soon appears on the L.

⑩ (12.4 km / 7.7 mi)   Cross Center Road, keeping to Hummel Lake Road. (Access to the lake is on your L at this intersection.)

⑪ (13.6 km / 8.4 mi)   At the next stop sign, turn R onto Fisherman Bay Road and then first L onto Lopez Road, and ride back to the village park.

- *Home with tower.*

SHAW ISLAND

SIZE: 21 km² (8 mi²)

POPULATION: 240

INFORMATION: www.visitsanjuanislands.com,
www.shawislanders.org

Before 2004 Franciscan nuns greeted visitors to Shaw Island
from the ferry. The order ran both the ferry terminal and
the adjacent general store. When you left the island, you'd
be given a blessing by the same nuns. If it sounds like Shaw
Island is peopled by devotees, you're about right. There are
two Catholic orders on the island (there used to be three):
the cloistered Benedictine nuns and the Sisters of Mercy. But
even for the non-believer, the island is a quiet, almost rustic
retreat, its simplicity and charm slowing the most energetic
of riders. The local school and museum are almost kitty-
corner from each other and are two of the oldest buildings on
all the islands. They are both designated historical sites, and
the school, known as the "little red school," built in 1890, is
the longest-running school in Washington State.

• *Busy Shaw Island!*

SHAW ISLAND ROUTE 15

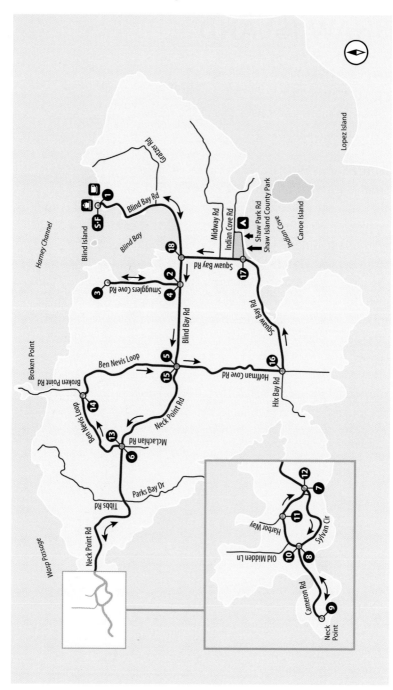

Tour of the Island

Of all the islands in this book, none is more sensitive to ferry schedules than Shaw Island. Times of arrival and departure will dictate how long you spend there and where you choose to linger. In any event, this route around such a lovely island will give you a good taste of what tranquility on the road can really be like. (Remember, the only accommodation available to you on the island is your tent – and space for that is very limited.)

DISTANCE	26 km/16 mi
LEVEL	Easy to moderate
HIGHLIGHTS	General store; Blind Bay; Neck Point isthmus; historic schoolhouse; library/museum; Benedictine Priory; Shaw Island County Park
START	Ferry terminal/general store

The Route

①   From the ferry terminal, you immediately pass the island's general store on your L and climb the Blind Bay Road hill.

② (2.3 km / 1.4 mi)   Having passed the community hall on the L, turn R onto Smugglers Cove Road. This is an out-and-back route, offering nice views over Blind Bay.

③ (3.7 km / 2.3 mi)   At the end of Smugglers Cove Road, retrace the route to Blind Bay Road.

④ (5.1 km / 3.2 mi)   Turn R onto Blind Bay Road.

⑤ (6.3 km / 3.9 mi)   Continue past the junction of Ben Nevis Loop, R, and Hoffman Cove Road, L, onto Neck Point Road.

⑥ (8.1 km / 5.0 mi)   Pass Ben Nevis Loop's west end, R.

⑦ (10.7 km / 6.6 mi)   Turn L onto Sylvan Circle.

⑧ (11.2 km / 6.9 mi)   Turn L onto Cameron Road. Part of this roadway is an isthmus – a narrow stretch of land with beach access on both sides.

⑨ (11.8 km / 7.3 mi)   End of Cameron Road. Retrace the route to arrive at the next checkpoint.

⑩ (12.4 km / 7.7 mi)   Turn L onto Sylvan Circle.

⑪ (12.6 km / 7.8 mi)   Pass Harbor Way on your L, staying on Sylvan Circle.

⑫ (12.8 km / 7.9 mi)   Turn L onto Neck Point Road at the next intersection.

⑬ (15.4 km / 9.6 mi)   Turn L onto Ben Nevis Loop. McLachlan Road goes R.

⑭ (16.7 km / 10.4 mi)   Pass the gravelled Broken Point Road on your L. (This is a steep hill going down to Broken Point. There's no public access.)

⑮ (18.5 km / 11.5 mi)   Cross Blind Bay Road onto Hoffman Cove Road. The island's historic schoolhouse and library/museum are at this intersection. Hoffman is a good-surfaced gravel road. (Cedar Rock Biological Preserve is accessed off the end of this road.)

⑯ (20.3 km / 12.6 mi)   Turn L onto Squaw Bay Road. (The Benedictine monastery for women, Our Lady of the Rock, is on the L just before this junction.)

⑰ (22.3 km / 13.8 mi)   Pass Shaw Park Road and the entrance to Shaw Island County Park on your R. A little farther is Indian Cove Road, also on your R.

⑱ (24.1 km / 14.9 mi)   Turn R onto Blind Bay Road and ride the roughly 2 km / 1.2 mi back to the ferry terminal.

- *Shaw Island marina.*

A novel way to wait for the ferry. Galiano Island.

GULF ISLANDS

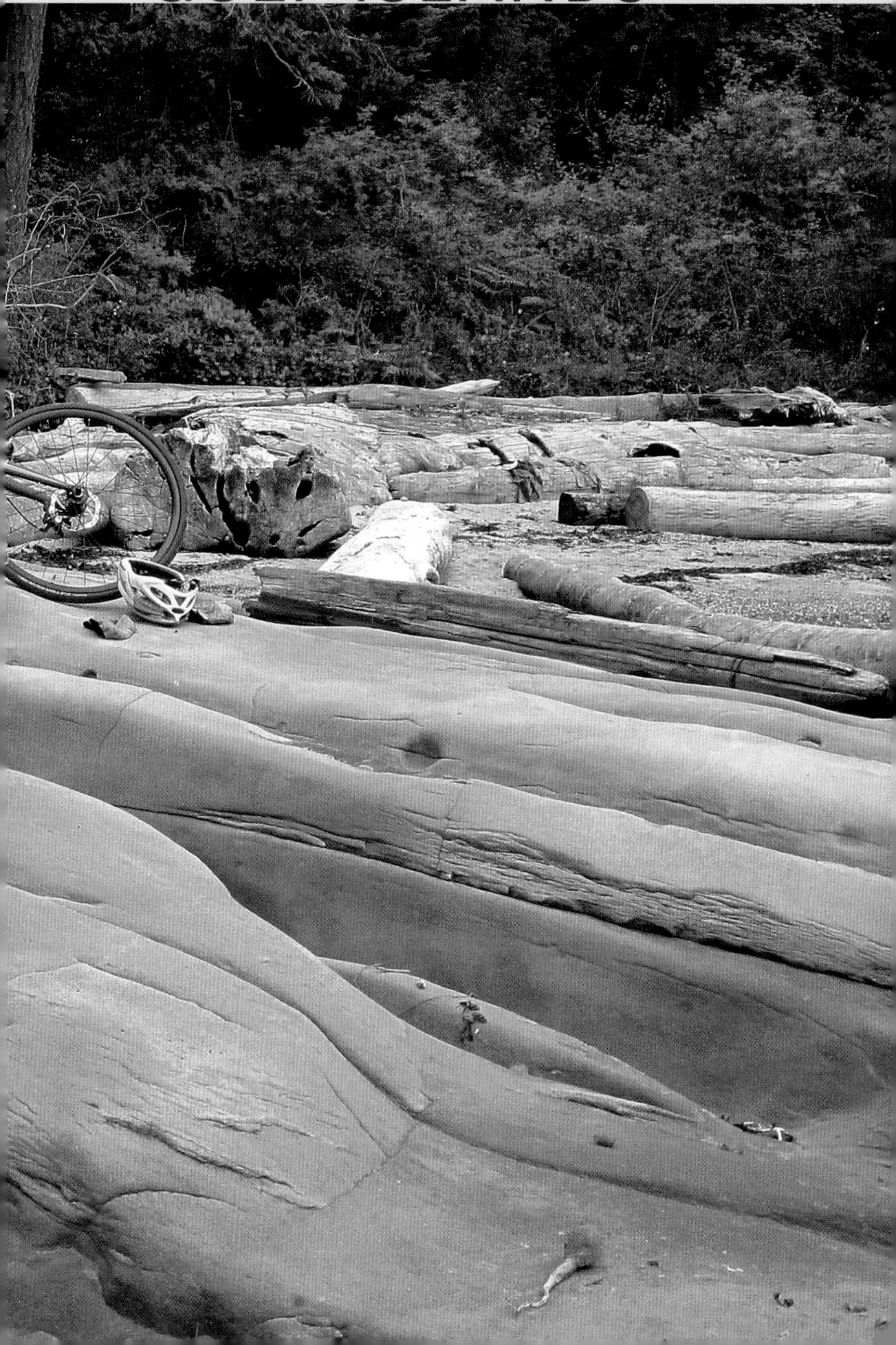

GULF ISLANDS

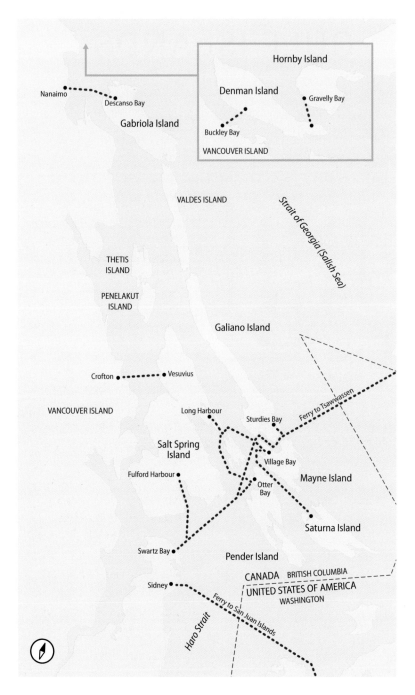

Hornby Island

Denman Island

Gravelly Bay

Buckley Bay

Gabriola Island

Nanaimo

Descanso Bay

VANCOUVER ISLAND

VALDES ISLAND

Strait of Georgia (Salish Sea)

THETIS
ISLAND

PENELAKUT
ISLAND

Galiano Island

Crofton   Vesuvius

Ferry to Tsawwassen

VANCOUVER ISLAND

Long Harbour

Sturdies Bay

Salt Spring
Island

Village Bay

Fulford Harbour

Otter
Bay

Mayne Island

Saturna Island

Swartz Bay

Pender Island

CANADA   BRITISH COLUMBIA

Sidney

UNITED STATES OF AMERICA
WASHINGTON

Ferry to San Juan Islands

Haro Strait

Introduction

The naming of the Gulf Islands was a mistake – a misnomer. In 1792, when Captain George Vancouver was exploring the southern reaches of Vancouver Island, he thought he was sailing in a body of water that had no exit, a dead end. He described it by the usual nautical term, a gulf. He was wrong. He was, in fact, navigating a strait – a stretch of water connecting two larger bodies of water like a sea or ocean. But the islands' name has stuck, their physical beauty and appeal reducing the name to a convenience.

For thousands of years the islands have been home to the indigenous peoples of the region. They are known as the Coast Salish First Nations and the most prolific residue of their occupation is middens – shell piles that surrounded their summer camps. (Today, the Tsawout First Nation has reserve land near Fulford Harbour.)

The Gulf Islands' modern history, while not as militaristic as the San Juans', is just as colourful. About the time the San Juans were being infiltrated by American and British troops, the southern Gulf Islands were experiencing their own influx of outsiders. The great gold rushes of the Cariboo and Fraser Canyon were at their height in the mid-1800s, and the Gulf Islands, situated as they are between Vancouver Island and the Fraser River, were a staging area for prospectors and hangers-on as they prepared to head north. Miners Bay on Mayne Island is a name from that era. The island built a jailhouse to cope with the occasional mayhem that the miners caused.

In the late 1850s Salt Spring Island became a haven for black Americans escaping racism. Australian, English, Hawaiian, Irish, Japanese, Portuguese, Scandinavian, and Scottish immigrants also made their way to the islands in the latter part of the 19th century, and vestiges of their homesteads and orchards are found almost everywhere. The 1960s saw many American men escaping to the islands to avoid the draft during the Vietnam War.

Spanish explorers of the area left their mark in the names they gave to islands, bays and bodies of water – just like in the San Juans. Galiano Island is named after the late-18th-century Spanish naval officer Dionisio Alcalá Galiano, as is the island's north-end marine park, Dionisio Point Provincial Park. Saturna Island is named after the Spanish vessel *Santa Saturnina*, captained, in 1791, by José María Narváez. His name is given to the island's lovely south-end bay. The Spanish word for seagull – *gaviota* – is thought to be at the root of Gabriola Island's name. The island's Malaspina Galleries and Descanso Bay also show its Spanish connections.

The more familiar British names of other islands come from naval officers of Royal Navy survey ships plying the area in the mid-1800s. Pender Island was named for Daniel Pender, a hydrographic surveyor on HMS *Plumper*. That vessel's captain, George Richards, named Mayne Island for his lieutenant, Richard Charles Mayne. Captain Richards also named Denman Island after another of his colleagues, Rear Admiral Joseph Denman. Hornby has a more complicated naming. The Spanish pipped the British in naming the island by over half a century. In 1791 the Spanish called the island Isla de Lerena. But in 1850 the British usurped the island's Spanish name, renaming it Hornby Island after one of its own explorers, Rear Admiral Phipps Hornby.

The Routes

SALT SPRING ISLAND

SIZE: 180 km² (70 mi²)

POPULATION: 10,500

INFORMATION: www.gulfislandstourism.com,
www.saltspringtourism.com, www.gulfislandsdriftwood.com

Salt Spring Island is the largest among the two island groups, and its community of Ganges is the only township on the Gulf Islands. The town's summer Saturday Market is the island's main attraction and has well over a hundred vendors selling artisanal goods and a large array of locally grown and produced foodstuffs. Ganges's plethora of other amenities makes it an obvious place to stop and visit.

The island has a number of lakes, the largest of which is St. Mary Lake on the north end. On the south end is the smaller Cusheon Lake. Both have public beach access and lakeside accommodation. The island's three provincial parks – Mount Maxwell, Burgoyne Bay and Ruckle – couldn't be more different from each other. Mount Maxwell is, well, just that – a mount. The road to its lookout at Baynes Peak is gravel and steep. But if you're keen to ride up (you can also hike), the views west over Vancouver Island and south to other Gulf islands and the San Juans are worth it. Burgoyne Bay Park is (as of this writing) in a rather embryonic stage. The shoreline is great, but there are no facilities and only a few trails. Ruckle Park, however, is one of the gems of the islands. It has an extensive shoreline and a network of trails that allows you to explore both the coast and the interior of the park. A plus is its picturesque waterfront walk-in campground.

• *Lonesome tent at Ruckle Park, Salt Spring Island.*

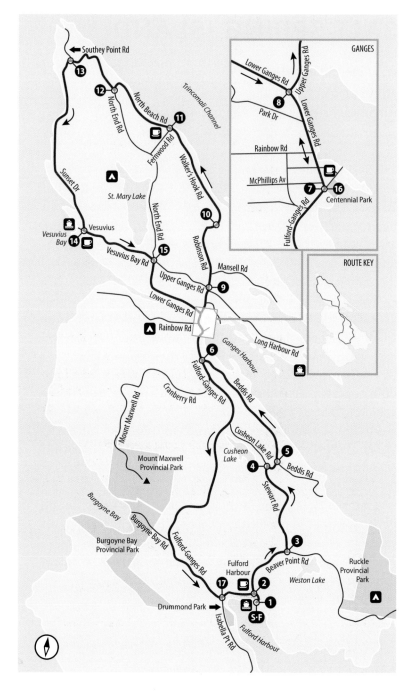

GANGES

ROUTE KEY

Southey Point Rd

North Beach Rd

Trincomali Channel

North End Rd

Fernwood Rd

Walker's Hook Rd

Sunset Dr

St. Mary Lake

Vesuvius
Bay

Vesuvius

Vesuvius Bay Rd

North End Rd

Robinson Rd

Mansell Rd

Upper Ganges Rd

Lower Ganges Rd

Rainbow Rd

Lower Ganges Rd

Park Dr

Upper Ganges Rd

Rainbow Rd

McPhillips Av

Fulford-Ganges Rd

Centennial Park

Long Harbour Rd

Ganges Harbour

Fulford-Ganges Rd

Cranberry Rd

Mount Maxwell Rd

Mount Maxwell
Provincial Park

Beddis Rd

Cusheon Lake Rd

Cusheon
Lake

Beddis Rd

Stewart Rd

Burgoyne Bay

Burgoyne Bay
Provincial Park

Burgoyne Bay Rd

Fulford-Ganges Rd

Fulford
Harbour

Beaver Point Rd

Weston Lake

Ruckle
Provincial
Park

Drummond Park

Isabella Pt Rd

Fulford Harbour

Tour of the Island

This route draws a large figure eight on the map of Salt Spring. The first few kilometres set the tone for this tour of the island – hilly and twisty. But there are flat and straight sections too, with one, Walker's Hook Road, paralleling the shore. Do not despair: the route is full of interest and the sights are worth all your efforts.

DISTANCE	55 km/34 mi
LEVEL	Moderate to strenuous
HIGHLIGHTS	Fulford Harbour; Ganges and Centennial Park Saturday Market; Walker's Hook Road and views over Galiano Island; Sunset Drive
START	Fulford Harbour ferry terminal

The Route

①		Leave the ferry terminal on Fulford–Ganges Road.
②	(0.2 km / 0.1 mi)	Turn R onto Beaver Point Road. (This is signed for Ruckle Provincial Park.) Pass Stowel Lake at 1.6 km (1.0 mi) on your R.
③	(2.8 km / 1.7 mi)	Turn sharply L onto Stewart Road. (For Ruckle Park, stay on Beaver Point Road, a further 7.0 km [4.3 mi].) Pass Peter Arnell Park on your R at 4.8 km (3.0 mi).
④	(6.3 km / 3.9 mi)	At the end of a long downhill, turn R onto the unsigned Cusheon Lake Road.
⑤	(7.1 km / 4.4 mi)	Turn L onto the unsigned Beddis Road.
⑥	(12.1 km / 7.5 mi)	Turn R onto Fulford–Ganges Road.

⑦ (13.2 km / 8.2 mi)   You are now in Ganges, the island's main centre. With Centennial Park on your R, turn L onto Lower Ganges Road.

⑧ (13.9 km / 8.6 mi)   At the north edge of the town, turn R onto Upper Ganges Road. (Pass Long Harbour Road on the R at 14.8 km [9.2 mi]. This 6.0-km [3.7-mi] road ends at the BC Ferries Terminal, where ferries depart for Vancouver.)

⑨ (15.0 km / 9.3 mi)   Bear R onto Robinson Road. To the L is Upper Ganges Road.

⑩ (17.0 km / 10.6 mi)   Curve R as Robinson becomes Walker's Hook Road. (At the top of a 14 per cent hill!)

⑪ (22.0 km / 13.7 mi)   Pass a government wharf on your R, with views over Galiano Island. To the L is Fernwood Road. (A coffee stop, if you like.) Walker's Hook now becomes North Beach Road.

⑫ (25.0 km / 15.5 mi)   Turn R onto North End Road.

⑬ (26.6 km / 16.5 mi)   With Southey Point Road on your R, bear L as North End Road becomes Sunset Drive.

⑭ (34.2 km / 21.2 mi)   Turn L onto Vesuvius Bay Road. (A café is just to the R, and the Vesuvius Bay Ferry Terminal is 0.5 km [0.3 mi] away, also to the R.)

⑮ (37.2 km / 23.1 mi)   At the four-way junction, turn R onto Lower Ganges Road.

⑯ (40.9 km / 25.4 mi)   Back in Ganges, turn R onto Fulford–Ganges Road. (Pass: Beddis Road, L, at 42 km [26.1 mi]; Cranberry Road, leading to Mount Maxwell Provincial Park, R, at 42.5 km [26.4 mi]; Cusheon

Lake Road – a possible route to Ruckle Park, L, at 45 km [28 mi]; and Burgoyne Bay Road to Burgoyne Bay Provincial Park, R, at 50 km [31 mi].)

⑰ (53.5 km / 33.2 mi) Bear L to Fulford Harbour. The ferry terminal is 1.5 km (0.9 mi) away. To the R is the mostly gravel road to Isabella Point.

• *Fulford Harbour with Mount Maxwell, Salt Spring Island.*

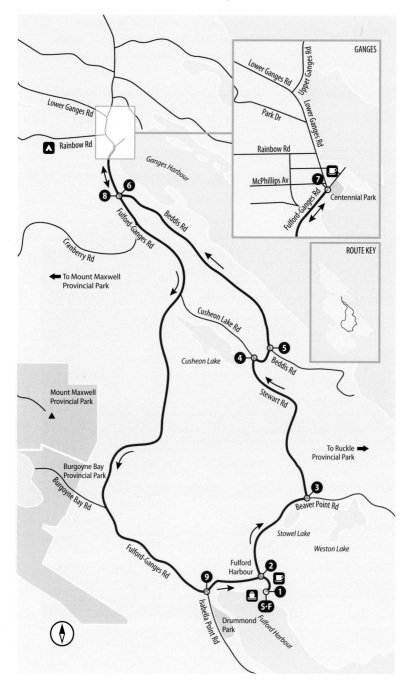

GANGES

Lower Ganges Rd

Upper Ganges Rd

Lower Ganges Rd

Park Dr

Rainbow Rd

McPhillips Av

7

Centennial Park

Fulford-Ganges Rd

ROUTE KEY

Lower Ganges Rd

Rainbow Rd

Ganges Harbour

Fulford-Ganges Rd

Beddis Rd

Cranberry Rd

◀ To Mount Maxwell
Provincial Park

Cusheon Lake Rd

Cusheon Lake

5

4

Beddis Rd

Mount Maxwell
Provincial Park

▲

Stewart Rd

To Ruckle ➡
Provincial Park

Burgoyne Bay
Provincial Park

Burgoyne Bay Rd

3

Beaver Point Rd

Stowel Lake

Weston Lake

Fulford-Ganges Rd

Fulford
Harbour

2

9

1

S·F

Isabella Point Rd

Drummond
Park

Fulford Harbour

8

6

Fulford-Ganges Rd

Lower Island Loop
(Ruckle Provincial Park an Option)

Apart from Beddis Road, this route is quite hilly, so be prepared for some grunt work. If you're making for Ruckle Provincial Park to either visit or camp, after the first couple of kilometres, bear R to keep to Beaver Point Road, the only road to the park.

DISTANCE	28 km/17 mi
LEVEL	Moderate to strenuous
HIGHLIGHTS	Stowel Lake; Ruckle Provincial Park; Ganges and Centennial Park Saturday Market; side trips to Burgoyne Bay or Mount Maxwell Provincial Park (both on gravel roads with the one to the latter being very steep); Fulford Harbour
START	Fulford Harbour ferry terminal

The Route

①   Leave the ferry terminal on Fulford–Ganges Road.

② (0.2 km / 0.1 mi)   Turn R onto Beaver Point Road. (This is signed for Ruckle Provincial Park.) Pass Stowel Lake on your R at 1.6 km (1.0 mi).

③ (2.8 km / 1.7 mi)   Turn sharply L onto Stewart Road. (For Ruckle Park, continue on Beaver Point Road for another 7 km [4.3 mi] – a straightforward ride.) Pass Peter Arnell Park at 4.8 km (3.0 mi).

④ (6.3 km / 3.9 mi)   At the first junction, turn R onto the unsigned Cusheon Lake Road.

⑤ (7.1 km / 4.4 mi)   Turn L onto the unsigned Beddis Road.

⑥ (12.1 km / 7.5 mi)   After a short rise, turn R onto Fulford–Ganges Road.

⑦ (13.2 km / 8.2 mi)   You are now in the town of Ganges, the island's main centre. This is your turnaround point.

⑧ (14.1 km / 8.7 mi)   Riding up the hill leaving the town, you pass Beddis Road on your L. As you continue your ride back to Fulford Harbour (including a long downhill) you'll also pass: Cranberry Road, R, a mostly gravel road up to Mount Maxwell Provincial Park at 14.6 km (9.0 mi); Cusheon Lake Road, L, a possible route to Ruckle Park at 17.2 km (10.7 mi); Burgoyne Bay Road, R, a gravel road to Burgoyne Bay Provincial Park at 23.2 km (14.4 mi).

⑨ (25.6km / 15.9 mi)   Bear L to Fulford Harbour, 1.5 km (0.9 mi) away. To the R is the road to Isabella Point.

- *Walk-in campground at Ruckle Park, Salt Spring Island.*
- *Enjoying the downhill.*

• *End of camping season, Ruckle Park, Salt Spring Island.*

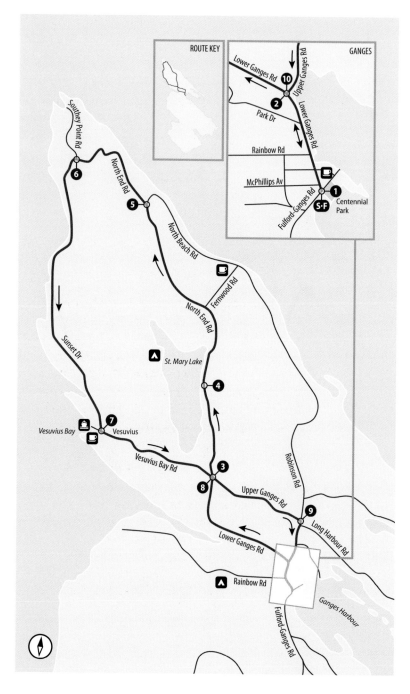

ROUTE KEY

GANGES

Lower Ganges Rd

Upper Ganges Rd

⑩

②

Park Dr

Lower Ganges Rd

Rainbow Rd

McPhillips Av

Fulford-Ganges Rd

①

S·F

Centennial Park

Southey Point Rd

⑥

North End Rd

⑤

North Beach Rd

Fernwood Rd

North End Rd

Sunset Dr

St. Mary Lake

④

Vesuvius Bay

⑦

Vesuvius

Vesuvius Bay Rd

③

⑧

Upper Ganges Rd

Robinson Rd

⑨

Long Harbour Rd

Lower Ganges Rd

Rainbow Rd

Fulford-Ganges Rd

Ganges Harbour

Upper Island Loop 1 *(Via St. Mary Lake)*

This is the least hilly excursion into the northern reaches of the island you'll get, and the only water you'll see is of St. Mary Lake (unless you visit Southey Point or Vesuvius Bay Terminal). The views over the farmland along Sunset Drive make up for the lack of ocean sights.

DISTANCE	26.5 km/16.5 mi
LEVEL	Moderate
HIGHLIGHTS	St. Mary Lake; Southey Point; Sunset Drive; Vesuvius Bay
START	Centennial Park, Ganges

The Route

① From the park, pass the fire hall and take Lower Ganges Road going out of town.

② (0.6 km / 0.4 mi) Bear L, keeping to Lower Ganges Road as Upper Ganges Road goes R.

③ (3.7 km / 2.3 mi) Cross the four-way intersection and continue straight on North End Road.

④ (5.7 km / 3.5 mi) St. Mary Lake beach accesses for the next 0.5 km (0.3 mi) on the L.

⑤ (10.3 km / 6.4 mi) Pass North Beach Road on your R.

⑥ (12.9 km / 8.0 mi) Southey Point Road on your R – a 1.5-km (0.9-mi) road to a sheltered bay and beach access. North End Road becomes Sunset Drive here.

⑦ (19.5 km / 12.1 mi) Turn L onto Vesuvius Bay Road. (A café is just to your R, and Vesuvius Bay Ferry Terminal is also to the R, 0.5 km [0.3 mi] away.)

⑧ (22.5 km / 14.0 mi) At the four-way intersection, continue straight on Upper Ganges Road.

⑨ (25.1 km / 15.6 mi) Turn R at the junction with Robinson Road to continue on Upper Ganges Road.

⑩ (26.0 km / 16.1 mi) Turn L onto Lower Ganges Road and ride the short distance back into Ganges.

• *Bike shop in Ganges, Salt Spring Island.*

19

Upper Island Loop 2
(Via Walker's Hook Road)

While much hillier than Route 18, this ride takes you along the picturesque Walker's Hook Road. Though not a long road, its proximity to the shore makes hopping off your bike and exploring the beach an easy and inviting prospect. The bucolic Sunset Drive, in complete contrast to Walker's Hook's shoreline views, seems just as pleasing.

DISTANCE	28 km/17.4 mi
LEVEL	Moderate to strenuous
HIGHLIGHTS	Walker's Hook Road; Southey Point; Sunset Drive; Vesuvius Bay Terminal
START	Centennial Park, Ganges

The Route

①		From the park, ride north on Lower Ganges Road.
②	(0.7 km / 0.4 mi)	At the edge of the village, turn R onto Upper Ganges Road.
③	(1.8 km / 1.1 mi)	Bear R onto Robinson Road. Upper Ganges Road continues L here.
④	(3.8 km / 2.4 mi)	Cresting a steep hill, Robinson swings R to become Walker's Hook Road.
⑤	(8.8 km / 5.5 mi)	Pass a government wharf on your R and Fernwood Road (with its café) on the L. Walker's Hook now becomes North Beach Road.
⑥	(11.8 km / 7.3 mi)	Turn R onto North End Road.
⑦	(13.4 km / 8.3 mi)	Pass Southey Point Road on your R – a pleasant detour. A kilometre (0.6 mi) after Southey, North End becomes Sunset Drive.

SALT SPRING ISLAND ROUTE 19

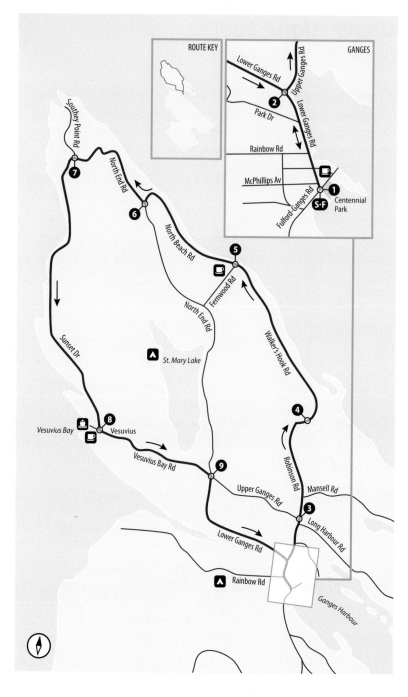

ROUTE KEY

GANGES

Lower Ganges Rd

Upper Ganges Rd

Park Dr

❷

Lower Ganges Rd

Rainbow Rd

McPhillips Av

Fulford-Ganges Rd

❶

S·F

Centennial Park

Southey Point Rd

❼

North End Rd

❻

North Beach Rd

❺

North End Rd

Fernwood Rd

Walker's Hook Rd

St. Mary Lake

Sunset Dr

❹

Robinson Rd

❽

Vesuvius Bay

Vesuvius

Vesuvius Bay Rd

❾

Upper Ganges Rd

Mansell Rd

❸

Long Harbour Rd

Lower Ganges Rd

Rainbow Rd

Ganges Harbour

⑧ (21.0 km / 13.0 mi) Turn L onto Vesuvius Bay Road. (A café is just to the R, and a little farther (0.5 km [0.3 mi]) along is the Vesuvius Bay Ferry Terminal.)

⑨ (24.0 km / 14.9 mi) At the four-way intersection, turn R onto Lower Ganges Road and ride the 3.7 km (2.3 mi) back to Ganges.

• *Ganges Harbour, Salt Spring Island.*

GALIANO ISLAND

SIZE: 57 km² (22 mi²)

POPULATION: 1,150

INFORMATION: www.gulfislandstourism.com,
www.galianoisland.com

Galiano is the slenderest of all the islands in the archipelago, its graceful body stretching almost 30 km (18 mi) from the shores of Sturdies Bay to Porlier Pass. Along the way is Montague Harbour, part of a provincial park, which has a walk-in campground and a white sandy beach. The island's three high points – Mount Galiano, Bluff Park and Bodega Ridge – are accessible by well-maintained trails. All have great views over water, islands and mountains.

An early white settler, Henry Georgeson, was a man who knew about islands. Born and raised on the largest of Scotland's Shetland Islands, he left to seek his fortune in lands far away. After he made some money in the Cariboo gold rush, he bought land on Galiano and settled down. (Sort of – he was the first lighthouse keeper for Mayne Island's Georgina Point lighthouse and spent 35 years there.) His land encompassed part of what is now Georgeson Bay. He died on the island in 1927, aged 92.

• *Only on the islands.*

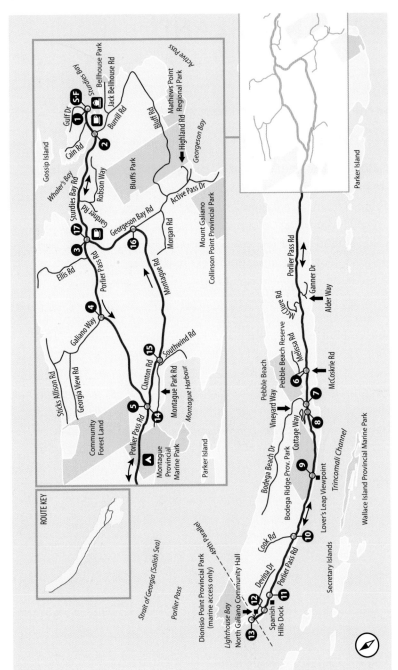

Sturdies Bay to North Galiano

20

Given the shape of the island, this route is inevitably an out-and-back. The island roads have their fair share of hills, but there are long stretches where you can put your mind, heart, lungs and legs in semi-neutral and let your eyes wander. In fact, the main road on this ride, Porlier Pass Road, is the longest and straightest road on all the islands, and you're on it for close to 23 km (14 mi). The views to the west are of Salt Spring, Wallace and Penelakut islands. There are two opportunities to hike on this route. One is along Bodega Ridge in Bodega Ridge Provincial Park. The trailhead is at the end of Cottage Way – a steep, 1-km (0.6-mi) climb from Porlier Pass Road. The other is Pebble Beach, which has a far more accessible trailhead at the end of the short, flat McCoskrie Road. A must while on Galiano is a visit is Montague Harbour Marine Provincial Park. You ride close to its entrance on your return journey.

DISTANCE	53 km/33 mi
LEVEL	Moderate to strenuous
HIGHLIGHTS	Sturdies Bay; views of Salt Spring Island; Pebble Beach Reserve; Bodega Ridge Provincial Park; Montague Harbour Marine Provincial Park
START	Sturdies Bay ferry terminal

The Route

①		Leave the ferry terminal on Sturdies Bay Road.
②	(0.5 km / 0.3 mi)	Bear R and continue on Sturdies Bay Road.
③	(2.8 km / 1.7 mi)	Turn R onto Porlier Pass Road. (Georgeson Bay Road goes L.)
④	(4.5 km / 2.8 mi)	Bear L, keeping to Porlier Pass Road. (Galiano Way goes R.)

⑤	(6.6 km / 4.1 mi)	Keep to Porlier Pass Road as it sweeps R past the junction with Clanton Road on the L. Clanton Road leads to Montague Harbour Marine Provincial Park.
⑥	(15.4 km / 9.6 mi)	To the R is McCoskrie Road – a 1-km-(0.6-mi-) long gravel road to Pebble Beach Reserve and beach trailhead.
⑦	(16.7 km / 10.4 mi)	On the R is Vineyard Way, which leads to Bodega Beach Road – a 6-km (3.7-mi) paved road to an isolated beach access.
⑧	(19.9 km / 12.4 mi)	Again on the R is Cottage Way – a steep, switchback (but paved) road – which leads to the trailhead into Bodega Ridge Provincial Park.
⑨	(18.8 km / 11.7 mi)	Lovers' Leap viewpoint over Salt Spring Island on your L.
⑩	(22.0 km / 13.7 mi)	Cook Road is on your R. This is a gravel road ending at private property, not a trailhead.
⑪	(25.0 km / 15.5 mi)	Spanish Hills dock on your L.
⑫	(25.3 km / 15.7 mi)	North Galiano Community Hall on your R.
⑬	(25.7 km / 16.0 mi)	Your outward route ends at Devina Drive – a dead-end gravel road going to the R.
⑭	(44.8 km / 27.8 mi)	On your return, turn R onto Clanton Road (signed for Montague Park).
⑮	(45.8 km / 28.5 mi)	If you're visiting the park, turn R here onto Montague Park Road. (The park is 1.5 km [1.0 mi] away.) Otherwise, continue east on the road, now named Montague Road.

⑯ (48.8 km / 30.3 mi) At a sweeping L bend, Montague joins Georgeson Bay Road coming in from the R.

⑰ (50.0 km / 31.1 mi) Turn R at the next junction (there's a market, liquor store and pub here) onto Sturdies Bay Road, and cycle the 3 km (1.9 mi) back to the ferry terminal.

• *Sturdies Bay ferry terminal.*

South Island Loop

Albeit a short ride, this loop takes you into an interesting, lumpy and forested part of the island. Bluff Road is narrow, gravelled and hilly for half its length, but it's lots of fun. "The Bluffs" trailhead is easily accessed from this road, and a Mount Galiano trailhead is not far away off Georgeson Bay Road.

DISTANCE	10 km/6 mi
LEVEL	Moderate to strenuous (suitable for sturdy touring bikes and mountain bikes)
HIGHLIGHTS	Bluff Road; "The Bluffs" trail; a Mount Galiano trail; the shore of Bellhouse Provincial Park
START	Sturdies Bay ferry terminal

The Route

① Leave the ferry terminal entrance on Sturdies Bay Road.

② (0.5 km / 0.3 mi) Turn L onto Burrill Road. (Soon after the turn, notice Jack Road on your L, which leads to Bellhouse Road and tiny Bellhouse Provincial Park.)

③ (2.0 km / 1.2 mi) Burrill bears abruptly R to become Bluff Road.

④ (3.0 km / 1.8 mi) At Warbler Road South (on your R), Bluff Road becomes a narrow, gravel and hilly road suitable only for mountain bikes and sturdy touring bikes.

⑤ (4.6 km / 2.8 mi) The trailhead to "The Bluffs" is on your R.

⑥ (5.1 km / 3.2 mi) Turn R onto Georgeson Bay Road. A trailhead to Mount Galiano is 100 m after the turn on your L.

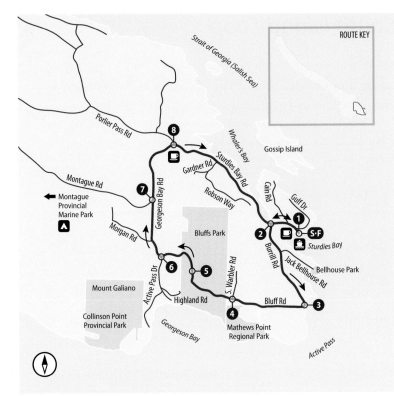

⑦ (6.1 km / 3.8 mi) Stop sign at the junction with Montague Road. Continue straight on Georgeson Bay Road.

⑧ (7.3 km / 4.5 mi) Turn R onto Sturdies Bay Road and ride the 3 km (1.8 mi) back to the ferry terminal.

• *Walk-in camping in Montague Park, Galiano Island.*

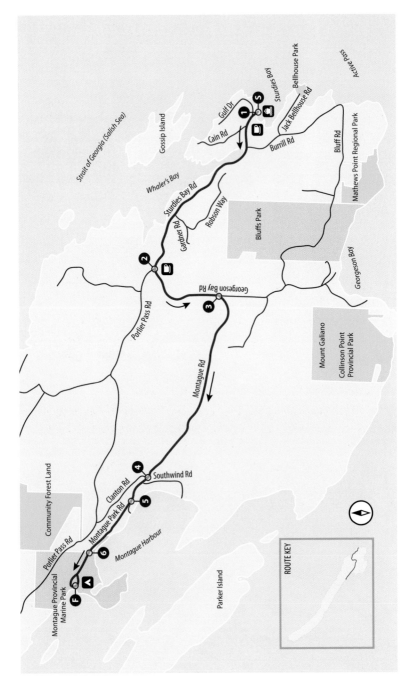

Ferry Terminal to Montague Harbour Marine Provincial Park

This route is primarily for those who intend to camp at Montague Park and want to set up before exploring the island. There's a market at the junction of Sturdies Bay and Georgeson Bay roads.

DISTANCE	8.3 km/5.1 mi
LEVEL	Moderate
START	Sturdies Bay ferry terminal

The Route

①   Leave the terminal on Sturdies Bay Road.

② (2.8 km / 1.7 mi)   Bear L onto Georgeson Bay Road. (Porlier Pass Road goes R.) At this junction you'll find a market, liquor store and pub.

③ (4.0 km / 2.5 mi)   Turn R onto Montague Road.

④ (6.8 km / 4.2 mi)   As Clanton Road intersects Montague Road on your R, you continue straight on Montague.

⑤ (7.3 km / 4.5 mi)   After a park sign, turn R onto Montague Park Road.

⑥ (8.3 km / 5.2 mi)   Enter the park.

PENDER ISLAND

Size: 36 km² (14 mi²)
Population: 2,250
Information: www.gulfislandtourism.com,
www.penderislandchamber.com

Pender is officially known as the Pender Islands, but in reality all that separates the two landmasses is a narrow, human-made channel traversed by a short bridge. Essentially, the two are one island. And that's how most people regard the place. It's one of the hilliest of the Gulf Islands from a cyclist's point of view, but its 244-m (800-ft) Mount Norman (which dominates the southern part of the island), can only be climbed on foot – thank goodness. Along with Beaumont Marine Park, the mount is part of the Gulf Islands National Park Reserve, which has large swathes of the island under its protection. Another large portion of the reserve includes Roesland and Roe Lake, both not far from the ferry terminal. While not as easily accessible or as developed as other parts of the reserve, Greenburn Lake, on the island's south end, is worth exploring. The hiking trail around the lake and to the park's western ridge are particularly rewarding.

The island's commercial hub is Driftwood Centre. Besides its large grocery store and pharmacy, it boasts both a liquor store and a book store – side by side. The only other quasi-commercial spot on the island is Hope Bay. Housed in a restored general store next to the government wharf are a café, an art gallery and a jeweller, as well as an assortment of other small businesses.

• *Canoe ride to Poets Cove, Pender Island.*

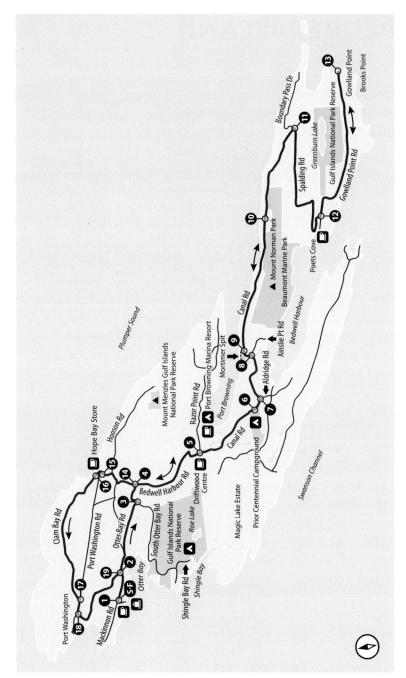

Tour of the Island

Though not an easy route, this ride will give you the satisfaction of having toured one of the most physically demanding islands, from a cyclist's point of view, in the entire archipelago. The route gives you a good taste of the whole island, its northern and southern parts, even though it omits one or two tentacles of roadways that are covered in the next two route descriptions. Luckily, there are four chances for liquid and food replenishment en route – Driftwood Centre, Port Browning, Poets Cove and Hope Bay. There's also the opportunity to ditch the bike for a while and hike up Mount Norman or down to Beaumont Marine Park and its secluded campsite.

DISTANCE	45.5 km/28.3 mi
LEVEL	Strenuous
HIGHLIGHTS	Driftwood Centre; Mount Norman and Beaumont Provincial Marine Park (hike only); Mortimer Spit; Poets Cove; Gowlland Point and Brooks Point; Hope Bay; Port Washington
START	Ferry terminal at Otter Bay

The Route

① Leave the terminal and cycle up the hill to join MacKinnon Road.

② (1.0 km / 0.6 mi) MacKinnon Road becomes Otter Bay Road, which rises from the L.

③ (2.4 km / 1.5 mi) Don't be alarmed by the signed T-junction with South Otter Bay Road, R. You have the right of way as the road turns abruptly L, then R. (South Otter Bay Road leads to the Shingle Bay walk-in/kayak campground, which has ten sites and is part of Gulf Islands National Park Preserve.)

④	(2.9 km / 1.8 mi)	Turn R onto Bedwell Harbour Road.
⑤	(5.0 km / 3.1 mi)	Driftwood Centre (stores and services) is on the R. Opposite is Razor Point Road, at the end of which is the road to Sea Star Vineyards. Shortly after the centre is Hamilton Road, L, leading down to Browning Harbour Marina's pub, café and campground. This is also the point where Bedwell Harbour Road becomes Canal Road.
⑥	(6.6 km / 4.1 mi)	Prior Centennial Campground is on your R.
⑦	(7.1 km / 4.4 mi)	Turn L onto a continuation of Canal Road.
⑧	(8.2 km / 5.1 mi)	Cross the bridge to South Pender, then turn L, keeping to Canal Road. (To turn R would lead to the trailhead to the high point on the island – Mount Norman – and to Beaumont Marine Park, both part of Gulf Islands National Park Reserve.)
⑨	(8.5 km / 5.3 mi)	Entrance to Mortimer Spit is on the L.
⑩	(10.7 km / 6.6 mi)	East entrance to Mount Norman Park, R.
⑪	(13.7 km / 8.5 mi)	Turn sharp R onto Spalding Road.
⑫	(16.9 km / 10.5 mi)	On the R is the steep hill down to Poets Cove Resort and Bedwell Harbour. You continue L on Gowlland Point Road.
⑬	(20.3 km / 12.6 mi)	Road's end at Gowlland Point. There's beach access here to Brooks Point and great views of Mount Baker, the North Cascades and the San Juan Islands. Retrace the route to checkpoint 4.

⑭	(37.6 km / 23.4 mi)	Instead of turning L onto Otter Bay Road, continue straight on Bedwell Harbour Road, following the signs for Hope Bay. Just past the library and church on your L, turn sharply R, keeping to Bedwell Harbour Road.
⑮	(38.7 km / 24.0 mi)	Pass Port Washington Road on the L. (For a slightly shorter and less hilly ride, take this road to checkpoint 18.)
⑯	(38.9 km / 24.2 mi)	Turn L onto Clam Bay Road. Hope Bay is on the R, with a café and retail stores.
⑰	(42.2 km / 26.2 mi)	Turn R onto Port Washington Road.
⑱	(42.6 km / 26.5 mi)	Turn L onto Otter Bay Road. (Going straight leads you to Port Washington wharf, 400 m [440 yd] or so away.)
⑲	(44.5 km / 27.7 mi)	Turn R onto MacKinnon Road and ride the kilometre back to the ferry landing.

• *Channel between north and south Pender.*

• *Hope Bay, Pender Island.*

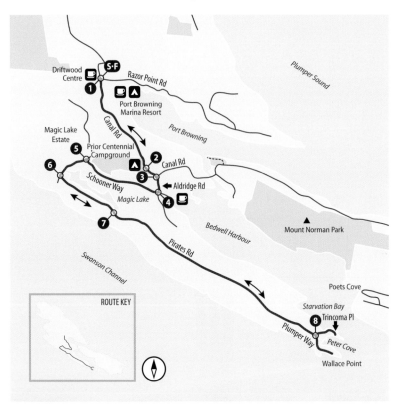

• *View south from Mount Norman, Pender Island.*

Starvation Bay, Peter Cove and Wallace Point

Pender's most populous enclave is the Magic Lake Estate subdivision on the southwestern part of the north island. Although its labyrinthine nature precludes inclusion in this book, this route does traverse part of it to travel along one of the flatter roads on the island to Wallace Point, Starvation Bay and Peter Cove. (If you do poke your nose into Magic Lake Estate, be prepared for lots of hills, tight bends and confusion.)

DISTANCE	20 km/12 mi (return)
LEVEL	Moderate
HIGHLIGHTS	Medicine Beach; Magic Lake; Starvation Bay; Peter Cove; Wallace Point
START	Driftwood Centre parking area

The Route

①   From the parking area, turn R onto Bedwell Harbour Road. (Bedwell soon becomes Canal Road.)

② (1.6 km / 1.0 mi)   Pass Prior Centennial Campground on your R. (The campground is part of Gulf Islands National Park Reserve.)

③ (2.1 km / 1.3 mi)   As Canal Road turns sharply L, you continue to the R onto Aldridge Road.

④ (2.5 km / 1.5 mi)   After 400 m (440 yd), at the bottom of the steep hill, the roads turns abruptly R and becomes Schooner Way. The road down to Medicine Beach is on the L at this corner. A store and café are also here.

⑤ (3.9 km / 2.4 mi)   Turn L at the fire hall to stay on Schooner Way. Pass the public access to Magic Lake a few hundred metres up on your L.

⑥ (4.5 km / 2.8 mi)   After the lake, turn L onto Pirates Road.

⑦ (5.6 km / 3.5 mi)   Entrance to Magic Lake swimming hole on your L.

⑧ (9.6 km / 6 mi)   At the end of a 4-km (2.5-mi) straightaway, bear L onto Bedwell Drive, then R onto Trincoma Place, and ride down to Starvation Bay. If you bear R at the end of Pirates Road onto Plumper Way, you'll reach Peter Cove and Wallace Point.

Retrace your route back to the Driftwood Centre.

• *Brooks Point in background, from Gowlland Point on Pender Island.*

Northend Loop
(Hope Bay and Port Washington)

Despite this being one of the shorter routes in the book, it won't disappoint. It goes without saying it's hilly, and one part, Clam Bay Road, is also quite narrow. Hope Bay, with its café, stores and government dock, is very attractive. Not far away is Port Washington, another charming spot. It has an abandoned general store, a government dock and a fine view over Swanson Channel to Prevost Island.

DISTANCE	13 km/8 mi
LEVEL	Moderate to strenuous
HIGHLIGHTS	Hope Bay; Clam Bay Road; Port Washington
START	Driftwood Centre parking area

The Route

①		From the parking area, turn L onto Bedwell Harbour Road.
②	(2.1 km / 1.3 mi)	Pass the community hall on your R and Otter Bay Road on your L.
③	(2.4 km / 1.5 mi)	Just past the library and a church on your L, turn sharply R onto a continuation of Bedwell Harbour Road.
④	(3.0 km / 1.9 mi)	Pass Port Washington Road on your L. (For a slightly shorter [2.0 km / 1.2 mi] and less hilly route, take Port Washington Road to checkpoint 7.)
⑤	(3.1 km / 1.9 mi)	Turn L onto Clam Bay Road. Hope Bay with its café, stores and dock is to the R as you turn the corner.
⑥	(6.5 km / 4.0 mi)	Turn R onto Port Washington Road.

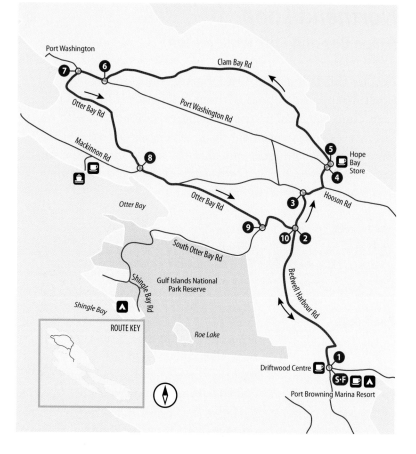

(7)	(6.8 km / 4.2 mi)	Turn L onto Otter Bay Road. (To ride to the Port Washington wharf, continue straight here for another 400 m [440 yd], after which it's down to your L.)
(8)	(9.5 km / 5.9 mi)	After passing through the golf course, turn L onto a continuation of Otter Bay Road.

• *Setting off from Gowlland Point, Pender Island.*

⑨ (10.9 km / 6.8 mi)   Pass South Otter Bay Road on your R.
                         You have the right of way as the road
                         swings L then R.

⑩ (11.2 km / 7.0 mi)   At the next junction, turn R onto
                         Bedwell Harbour Road and ride the
                         2.0 km (1.2 mi) back to Driftwood
                         Centre.

MAYNE ISLAND

SIZE: 21 km² (8.1 mi²)

POPULATION: 1,100

INFORMATION: www.gulfislandstourism.com,
www.mayneisland.com

Mayne Island's history is not only recalled by a jail convert-
ed into a museum but also by a beautiful, formal Japanese
garden at Dinner Bay, which memorializes its Japanese immigrants. More history is found at the decommissioned Georgina Point Lighthouse guarding the entrance to Active Pass,
which is now part of a heritage park, its grassy shorefront
making an ideal picnic spot. It was first manned in 1885 by
Henry Georgeson – who also lived on Galiano Island, as you'll
read.

Attesting to the fact that human needs, both physical
and spiritual, were and are not neglected on the island are
the Springwater Lodge at Miners Bay, where food and drink
are still served, and St. Mary Magdalene Anglican Church,
just around the corner, which holds services every Sunday
morning. Both were built in the 1890s.

There are no so-called harbours on Mayne, only bays.
And there are several. The largest is Campbell Bay on the
island's northeast side. The most secluded is Horton Bay on
its southeast side. You can visit both on the rides described
below.

• *Indigenous art at Horton Bay, Mayne Island.*

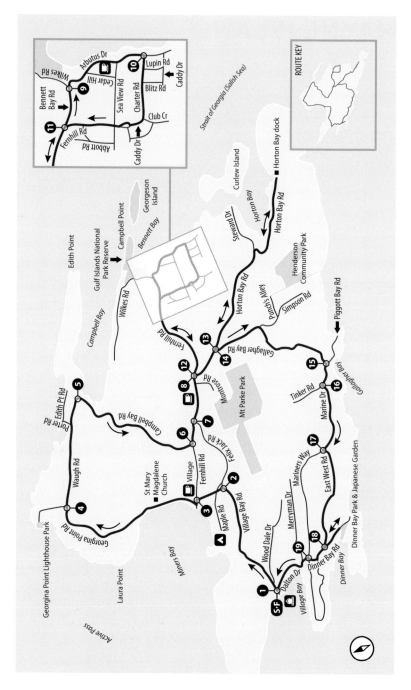

Tour of the Island

There's much to see on Mayne, even though it's the smallest of the Gulf Islands described in the book. This loop route takes you past the island's village centre, with its heritage museum and agricultural hall. You'll also pass a century-old church, a lighthouse, numerous farms, inviting beaches, a trail to the island's high point and a beautiful Japanese garden. But that's not all you'll discover cycling the sometimes lumpy roads of this interesting island.

DISTANCE	31 km/19 mi
LEVEL	Moderate to strenuous
HIGHLIGHTS	Miners Bay; Georgina Point Heritage Park and Lighthouse; Mount Parke Regional Park (hike); Campbell Point Park; Horton Bay dock; Dinner Bay Park and Japanese Garden
START	Village Bay ferry terminal

The Route

① Leave the ferry terminal, bearing L onto Village Bay Road.

② (3.0 km / 1.9 mi) Bear L as the road curves toward Miners Bay village centre. Felix Jack Road comes in from the R.

③ (3.8 km / 2.3 mi) In the village, turn L onto Fernhill Road then, at the dock, R onto Georgina Point Road, and ride along the shore of Miners Bay and past St. Mary Magdalene Anglican Church, R.

④ (5.5 km / 3.4 mi) As Georgina Point Road turns sharply L, you continue straight on Waugh Road. Georgina Point Heritage Park and Lighthouse are 0.5 km (0.3 mi) away down Georgina Point Road.

⑤ (7.5 km / 4.7 mi) At a long R curve, Waugh becomes Campbell Bay Road. On the L is a beach access to Campbell Bay.

⑥ (9.5 km / 5.9 mi) Turn L onto Fernhill Road.

⑦ (9.8 km / 6.1 mi) Pass Felix Jack Road and the island health centre on your R. (The next road on your R is Montrose Road. This short road leads to the trailhead for Mount Parke Park. A café, gallery, bookstore and market are also here.)

⑧ (10.5 km / 6.5 mi) Horton Bay Road junction is on the R. You continue on Fernhill until it turns abruptly R, while you go straight on Bennett Bay Road.

⑨ (12.3 km / 7.6 mi) Just before the road bends R to become Arbutus Drive, Wilkes Road goes to the L (and to Bennett Bay and Campbell Point Gulf Islands National Park Reserve land). You follow Arbutus.

⑩ (12.8 km / 7.9 mi) After passing a resort on your L, turn R onto Charter Road then R again onto Caddy Drive, which quickly becomes Fernhill Road.

⑪ (14.4 km / 8.9 mi) Turn L onto a continuation of Fernhill Road.

⑫ (15.8 km / 9.8 mi) Turn L onto Horton Bay Road.

⑬ (16.8 km / 10.4 mi) At the Horton Bay Road–Gallagher Bay Road junction, bear L, taking Horton Bay Road. This road terminates at secluded Horton Bay and its government dock. Return to the junction.

⑭ (23.2 km / 14.4 mi) Turn L onto Gallagher Bay Road.

• *On the way to Mayne Island – in the rain.*

⑮ (25.5 km / 15.8 mi)   At the bottom of a long hill, the road bears R to become Marine Drive. Piggott Bay Road is on the L and leads to a beach access.

⑯ (25.8 km / 16.0 mi)   Continue on Marine Drive as it turns sharply L. Tinker Road goes straight.

⑰ (27.0 km / 16.8 mi)   As Marine Drive becomes Mariners Way, look for and turn L onto East West Road.

⑱ (28.5 km / 17.7 mi)   East West Road intersects Dinner Bay Road. Turn L here and descend the hill to Dinner Bay Park and Japanese Garden. (The garden is worth a visit. Admission is by donation.) Return along Dinner Bay Road.

⑲ (30.0 km / 18.6 mi)   Turn R onto Mariners Way and then immediately L onto Dalton Drive – a steep downhill. This leads to the Village Bay ferry terminal, 1 km (0.6 mi) away and the ride's end.

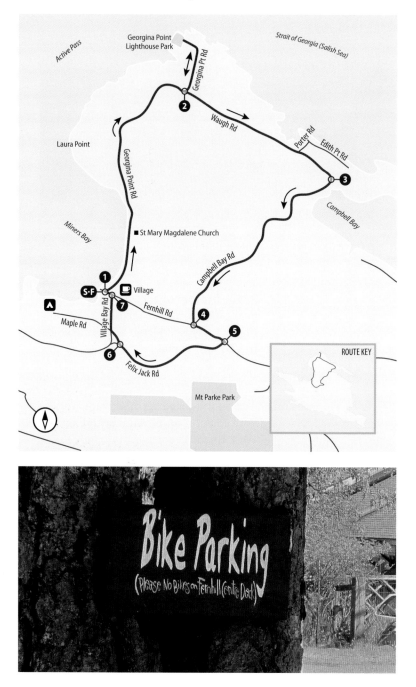

North Island Loop

This short loop is intended to show the way to one of Mayne Island's favourite spots – Georgina Point Heritage Park and Lighthouse. Built in 1885, the lighthouse, although no longer manned, serves to alert mariners of the tricky waters of Active Pass over which it stands guard. For those who enjoy a cooling dip on a hot day, the route also passes the sandy beach of Campbell Bay.

DISTANCE	9 km/5.6 mi
LEVEL	Moderate
HIGHLIGHTS	Georgina Point Heritage Park and Lighthouse; Campbell Bay beach
START	Entrance to Miners Bay dock

The Route

①   A few metres before the dock, turn R onto Georgina Point Road.

② (1.6 km / 1.0 mi)   Follow Georgina Point Road as it veers L down to Georgina Point Heritage Park and Lighthouse a short distance away. After your visit return to checkpoint 2 and turn L onto Waugh Road.

③ (4.6 km / 2.8 mi)   Waugh Road turns sharply R to become Campbell Bay Road. A beach access is soon signed on your L.

④ (6.6 km / 4.1 mi)   Turn L onto Fernhill Road.

⑤ (6.9 km / 4.3 mi)   Turn R onto Felix Jack Road. The island's community centre is on the R, a short way from the junction.

⑥ (8.0 km / 4.9 mi)   Bear R as Felix Jack joins Village Bay Road.

⑦ (8.8 km / 5.4 mi)   In the village, turn L onto Fernhill Road and ride back to the route's start at Miners Bay.

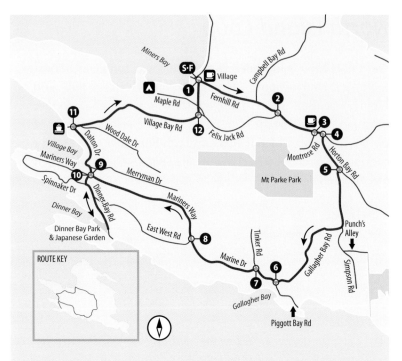

• *Farmland, Mayne Island.*

South Island Loop

First, the hard part. This route takes you along the hilliest roads on the island – Gallagher Bay Road, Marine Drive and Mariners Way. A masochist's delight. The upside is that you can visit the Japanese Garden at Dinner Bay Park and/or hike up Mt. Parke. Also, you can browse the bookstore, art gallery and farm market at Montrose Road corner before the pain of the hills begins.

DISTANCE	13 km/8 mi
LEVEL	Moderate to strenuous
HIGHLIGHTS	Dinner Bay Park and Japanese Garden; Horton Bay dock; hike up Mount Parke
START	Fernhill Road–Village Bay Road junction

The Route

①   From the junction, ride east along Fernhill Road (through the village).

② (1.7 km / 1.0 mi)   Pass Felix Jack Road on your R.

③ (2.2 km / 1.4 mi)   Pass Montrose Road (trailhead to Mount Parke Park), a café, farm market and stores on your R.

④ (2.4 km / 1.5 mi)   Turn R onto Horton Bay Road.

⑤ (3.4 km / 2.1 mi)   Bear R onto Gallagher Bay Road. (Horton Bay Road goes to the L and ends at the bay's dock 3.0 km [1.9 mi] away.)

⑥ (5.7 km / 3.5 mi)   Gallagher Bay Road bears R to become Marine Drive at the bottom of a steep hill.

⑦ (6.0 km / 3.7 mi)   Marine Drive turns sharply L. (Tinker Road goes straight ahead.)

⑧ (7.2 km / 4.5 mi)	Pass East West Road on your L. Keep to Marine Drive as it becomes Mariners Way.
⑨ (8.7 km / 5.4 mi)	Turn L onto Dinner Bay Road and descend to Dinner Bay Park and Japanese Garden. Retrace the route up to Mariners Way
⑩ (10.2 km / 6.3 mi)	Turn R onto Mariners Way then L onto Dalton Road and ride the steep downhill to the Village Bay ferry terminal entrance.
⑪ (10.9 km / 6.8 mi)	Turn R onto Village Bay Road.
⑫ (13.9 km / 8.6 mi)	Bear L as the road heads for Miners Bay. Felix Jack Road comes in from the R. In less than a kilometre (0.6 mi), you're back at the ride's start.

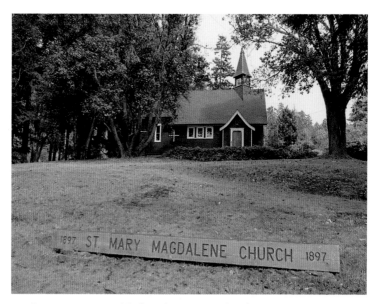

- **Above:** *Century-old church, Mayne Island.*
- *At the fair, Mayne Island.*

SATURNA ISLAND

SIZE: 31 square kilometres (12 square miles)

POPULATION: 350

INFORMATION: www.gulfislandtourism.com,
www.saturnaisland.com, www.saturnatourism.com/

About 50 per cent of Saturna Island is parkland and protected under Gulf Islands National Park Reserve. So it's sparsely populated and has plenty of space for animals and humans to roam around. At the end of each of the island's two finger-like main roads are a couple of the most beautiful spots on all the islands – Narvaez Bay and Echo Bay and East Point Park. The highest point on the island is Mount Warburton Pike, a 401-m (1,316-ft) peak. There are grand views from its summit (including the island's vineyard) and it is the trailhead for the spectacular Brown Ridge Nature Trail. Unfortunately, the only way to the top is via the steep, windy and gravel Staples Road, a 4-km (2.5-mi) slog that is not described here. Like many of the islands, Saturna caters to a thirsty cyclist by conveniently locating a pub next to the ferry terminal. (Inconveniently, it's only open during summer months.)

• *Cozy campground at Narvaez Bay, Saturna Island.*

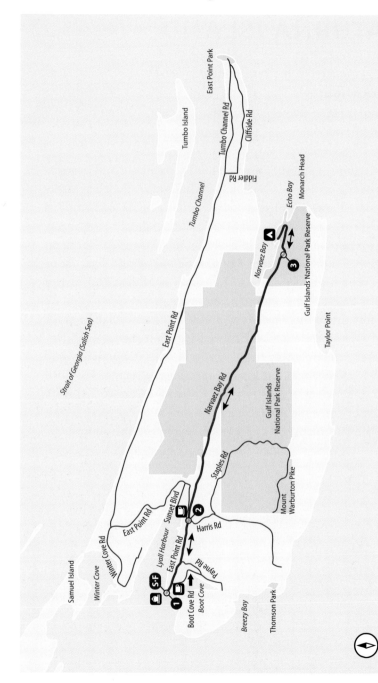

Narvaez Bay

The road to Narvaez Bay is not too long, not too straight and not too hilly. In fact, apart from being mostly gravel, it's a pleasant ride to reach three of the island's most picturesque spots: Echo Bay, Monarch Head and Narvaez Bay's campsite.

DISTANCE	22 km/13.7 mi (return)
LEVEL	Moderate (2/3 gravel)
HIGHLIGHTS	Echo Bay; Monarch Head; Narvaez Bay walk-in/kayak-in campsite (seven sites only)
START	Lyall Harbour ferry terminal

The Route

① From the ferry terminal, ride up East Point Road.

② (1.7 km / 1.0 mi) At the junction of East Point Road and Narvaez Bay Road, continue straight on Narvaez Bay Road. Saturna General Store and Café is on your L, just past the junction. (Harris Road is on the R and leads to Mount Warburton Pike and the island's winery.)

③ (11.5 km / 7.1 mi) After a slightly lumpy ride (on a mostly gravel surface), the road ends at the entrance to Narvaez Bay and Echo Bay trailhead, L. This 1.5-km (0.9-mi) trail ends at Narvaez Bay campsite; the promontory of Echo Bay is at 0.7 km (0.4 mi), on your R at the bottom of the hill. A trail to Monarch Head is near the top of the hill.

Return to the ferry terminal.

• *View from Monarch Head, south Saturna Island.*

East Point Park

After an initially hilly section to Winter Cove, East Point Road calms down and becomes a hospitable ride to the most easterly point of the Gulf Islands – East Point. The road affords numerous places to stop and walk on the rocky shoreline or to take in the views over the Salish Sea's Georgia Strait to Washington State (and Mount Baker, if the sky is clear).

DISTANCE	33 km/20.5 mi (return)
LEVEL	Easy to strenuous
HIGHLIGHTS	Winter Cove; East Point Park, lighthouse and restored Fog Alarm Building
START	Lyall Harbour ferry terminal

The Route

①   From the ferry terminal, ride up East Point Road to its junction with Narvaez Bay Road.

② (1.7 km / 1.0 mi)   Turn L onto the continuation of East Point Road. (Saturna Island General Store and Café is at this corner on Narvaez Bay Road.)

③ (3.7 km / 2.3 mi)   At the junction with Winter Cove Road, turn R onto the continuation of East Point Road. (Winter Cove Park is 0.5 km [0.3 mi] to the L.)

④ (13.7 km / 8.5 mi)   East Point Road becomes Tumbo Channel Road. (You can glimpse Tumbo Island through the trees.)

⑤ (16.7 km / 10.4 mi)   The road ends at the entrance to East Point Park and the lighthouse outbuildings. There are bike racks here if you want to explore the point on foot.

- *Echo Bay, Saturna Island.*

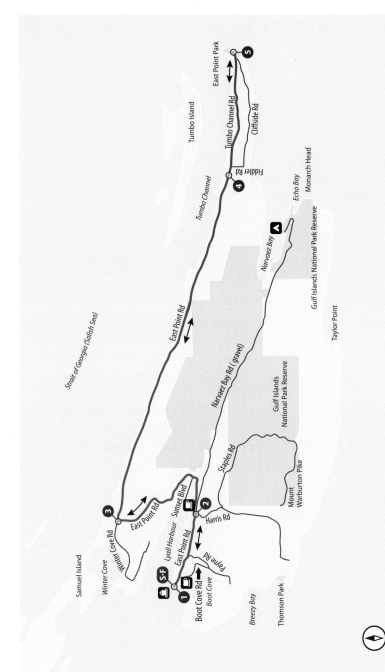

⑥ To return to the ferry terminal, take either Tumbo Channel Road or, upon leaving the park, turn L onto Cliffside Road, a crescent (and pleasant) road detour back to East Point Road.

• *Orcas Island's Mount Constitution from East Point Park, Saturna Island.*

GABRIOLA ISLAND

Size: 53 km² (20.5 mi²)
Population: 4,500
Information: www.gulfislandstourism.com,
www.gabriolaisland.org

Gabriola Island is the second largest Gulf Island by population, primarily due to its proximity to the city of Nanaimo – a stone's throw away. It's one of the easiest islands to cycle, with only a few major hills to climb. There are three waterfront provincial parks on the island, each quite different from the rest. The smallest, Gabriola Sands, is the most accessible, as it's only a couple of kilometres (1.2 mi) from the ferry terminal. Its two sandy beaches make ideal picnic spots. Sandwell is the next in size at 12 ha (30 ac). It's on the rock and sandy shore of Lock Bay and faces east to overlook the Salish Sea. Drumbeg is tucked away on the island's southeast end and has an appealing sense of seclusion the other two parks lack. The island's shoreline, predominantly sandstone, gives rise to some exotic shapes and forms. The Malaspina Galleries, rock formations at the island's northwest end, are dramatic examples.

Much of the island's commercial life is focused on the aptly named Folklife Village Shopping Centre, a short distance from the ferry terminal.

• *Gabriola Island's shopping mall.*

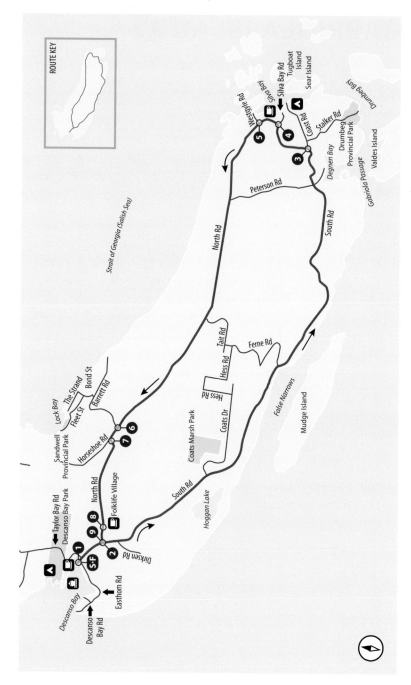

Tour of the Island

The contrast between South and North roads is quite distinct. While not devoid of trees, South Road is rather bucolic and, for a long stretch, has views west over Mudge Island and False Narrows. North Road is less developed, more forested and traverses the shady side of the island. On the southeastern end of the island is Drumbeg Provincial Park. This route passes close to its gravel access road and a detour is an easy ride. If you're inclined to be adventurous, there are plenty of opportunities on this tour of the island to poke your nose into its numerous side roads. You could even traverse its middle on Ferne and Tait roads.

DISTANCE	28 km/17.4 mi
LEVEL	Moderate to strenuous
HIGHLIGHTS	Views over Mudge Island and False Narrows from South Road; Drumbeg Provincial Park; Silva Bay Resort pub; Folklife Village
START	Descanso Bay ferry terminal

The Route

①   Climb the steep hill from the terminal on North Road for just over 0.5 km (0.3 mi).

② (0.6 km / 0.4 mi)   At the first major junction, North Road turns L. You continue straight onto South Road. (The island's main shopping area is a few hundred metres up North Road.)

③ (13.9 km / 8.6 mi)   Pass Coast Road, R. Take this road to visit Drumbeg Provincial Park and/or Page's Resort and Marina for camping and supplies. (The road to the park is gravel.)

④ (15.3 km / 9.5 mi)   Pass the entrance to Silva Bay Resort. (It has a pub, by the way.) Silva Bay is seen through the trees.

⑤ (15.5 km / 9.6 mi)   At Westgyle Road, R, South Road becomes North Road.

⑥ (24.6 km / 15.3 mi)   Barrett Road on the R is the access route to Sandwell Provincial Park, 2.0 km (1.2 mi) away.

⑦ (25.0 km / 15.5 mi)   Bear L to keep to North Road. Horseshoe Road goes straight.

⑧ (27.1 km / 16.8 mi)   Entrance to the island's shopping centre, Folklife Village, is on the L.

⑨ (27.5 km / 17.0 mi)   Turn R for the short downhill return to the ferry terminal.

● *But that's only downhill!*

Orlebar Point

Orlebar Point is famous for its views of the photogenic Entrance Island and its lighthouse. You might even have seen it from the deck of a BC Ferries vessel on your way from Horseshoe Bay to Nanaimo. This route takes you there. On the way, you'll pass Descanso Bay Regional Park, the road to the sandstone Malaspina Galleries and the small Gabriola Sands Provincial Park. The island's visitor centre is also on this route.

DISTANCE	11 km/6.8 mi (return)
LEVEL	Moderate
HIGHLIGHTS	Orlebar Point; Descanso Bay Regional Park; The Malaspina Galleries; Gabriola Sands Provincial Park
START	Descanso Bay ferry terminal

The Route

①		Shortly after leaving the ferry terminal, turn L onto Taylor Bay Road. (This is a busy junction for ferry traffic.)
②	(0.9 km /0.6 mi)	On the L is Descanso Bay Regional Park (and campground). Also on the L, and just before the next checkpoint, is Malaspina Drive, at the end of which are the Malaspina Galleries.
③	(2.0 km /1.2 mi)	Bear R onto Berry Point Road.
④	(2.2 km /1.4 mi)	On the R is the island's visitor centre. On the L, a short distance down Ricardo Road, is Gabriola Sands Provincial Park.

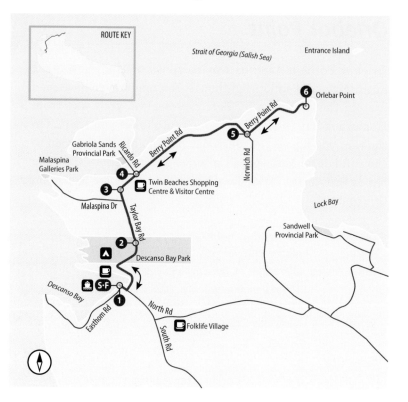

ROUTE KEY

Strait of Georgia (Salish Sea)   Entrance Island

Orlebar Point

Berry Point Rd

Norwich Rd

Gabriola Sands
Provincial Park

Ricardo Rd

Malaspina
Galleries Park

Lock Bay

Twin Beaches Shopping
Centre & Visitor Centre

Sandwell
Provincial Park

Malaspina Dr

Taylor Bay Rd

Descanso Bay Park

Descanso Bay

North Rd

Easthom Rd

South Rd

Folklife Village

⑤ (4.4 km / 2.7 mi) Watch for and turn L onto the
continuation of Berry Point Road.
(The steep hill straight ahead is
Norwich Road.)

⑥ (5.5 km / 3.4 mi) The paved road ends here, at Orlebar
Point. There are good views over
Entrance Island and its lighthouse
and the mainland beyond. Retrace
your ride to the route's start.

• *Entrance Island from Orlebar Point, Gabriola Island.*

DENMAN ISLAND AND HORNBY ISLAND

Denman Island
SIZE: 51 km² (19.7 mi²)
POPULATION: 1,100
INFORMATION: www.denmanisland.com

Hornby Island
SIZE: 30 km² (11.6 mi²)
POPULATION: 1,000
INFORMATION: www.realhornbyisland.com, www.hornbyisland.com

The sister islands Denman and Hornby sit in Baynes Sound, 2 km (1.2 mi) from the shores of Vancouver Island's Buckley Bay. Though sisters, they're not identical twins. Far from it. Though Hornby is roughly half the size of Denman, it has about the same population. And in summer, Hornby's population can quadruple, which is to say, it's a popular vacation spot. The 1-km- (0.6-mi-) long white sandy beach of Tribune Bay Provincial Park is a major draw, as is its neighbour, Ringside Market. Helliwell Provincial Park has a dramatic cliffedge trail – a trail that has no equal in all the archipelago.

Denman is more demure. Its public spaces are not too showy. You have to make an effort to visit its two provincial parks, Fillongley and Boyle Point (both worth it). It has a funky general store at the top of the ferry hill that is post office, liquor store and gas bar to boot. The cable ferry from the mainland to the island is the world's longest.

• *Hornby Island community hall's imposing entrance.*

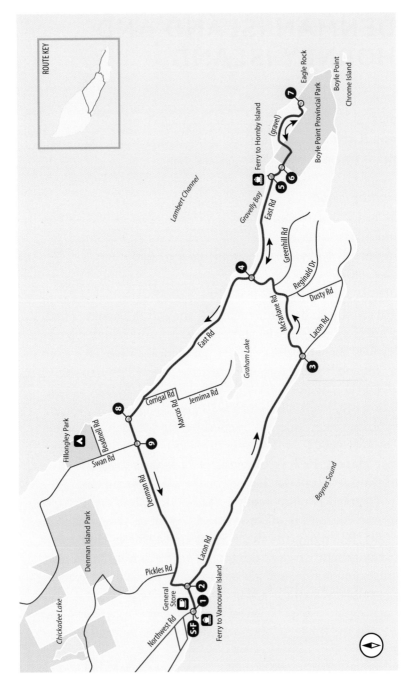

ROUTE KEY

Eagle Rock

Boyle Point

Chrome Island

Boyle Point Provincial Park

(gravel)

Ferry to Hornby Island

Gravelly Bay

East Rd

Greenhill Rd

Reginald Dr

Dusty Rd

Lambert Channel

McFarlane Rd

Lacon Rd

East Rd

Graham Lake

Baynes Sound

Corrigal Rd

Jemima Rd

Marcus Rd

Fillongley Park

Beadnell Rd

Swan Rd

Denman Rd

Denman Island Park

Chickadee Lake

Lacon Rd

Pickles Rd

General Store

S-F

Northwest Rd

Ferry to Vancouver Island

South Denman Island Loop
(Including Route to Hornby Island Ferry)

The anticlockwise direction of this loop route is deliberate – the reason for which you won't appreciate until you've almost finished the ride. I'll leave it at that. Denman Island is long and somewhat skinny, and is neatly divided in half by Denman Road. This route explores the island's southern half. One resident remarked that the island was roughly the size of Manhattan but had less than one one-thousandth of its population. So don't expect to see lots of people. In addition to two provincial parks, Denman has a nice mix of farmland, forest and exposed shoreline, and this ride reveals all three.

DISTANCE	28.5 km/17.7 mi
LEVEL	Moderate
HIGHLIGHTS	East Road shoreline; Boyle Point Provincial Park and Eagle Rock; Fillongley Provincial Park; Denman Island General Store
START	Denman Island General Store

The Route

①   From the store, ride the short distance to the junction of Denman and Northwest roads (top of the ferry hill). Turn L onto Denman Road.

② (0.6 km / 0.4 mi)   As the road forks, take the R fork onto Lacon Road.

③ (6.5 km / 4 mi)   After the flattish and straight Lacon Road, turn L onto the rolling, curving McFarlane Road.

④ (9.6 km / 6.0 mi)   Turn R onto East Road.

⑤ (11.9 km / 7.4 mi)   Pass the approach road to the Hornby Island ferry terminal, L.

⑥ (14.0 km / 8.7 mi) East Road becomes gravel after the ferry terminal and terminates at the entrance to Boyle Point Provincial Park. (There are bike racks here if you decide to visit Eagle Rock and/or Boyle Point. The latter has views over Chrome Island Lighthouse.)

⑦ (18.0 km / 11.2 mi) From Boyle Point, retrace your route to checkpoint 4 (McFarlane Road). Continue straight on East Road.

⑧ (23.0 m / 14.3 mi) East Road turns sharply L to become Denman Road.

⑨ (24.1 km / 15.0 mi) Pass Swan Road on your R. This road leads to Fillongley Provincial Park a short distance away. Denman Road takes you back (via a very steep but short downhill) to the route's start at the general store, 4.4 km (2.7 mi) away.

- **Above:** *Gravelly Bay Ferry Terminal.*
- **Right:** *Hornby Island through the trees.*

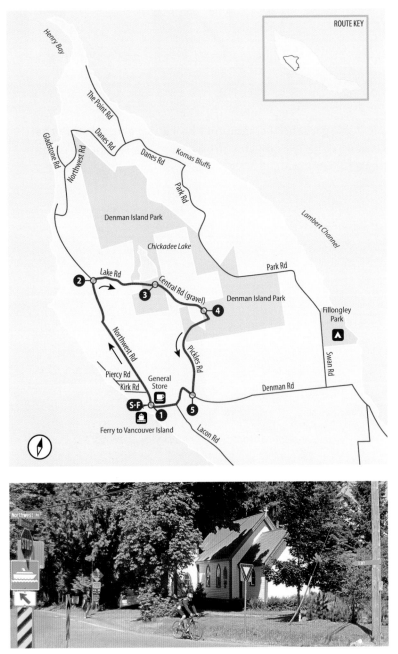

- *Top of the ferry hill, Denman Island.*

Northwest Road – Pickles Road Loop (Denman Island)

This short route will give you a glimpse into rural island life. Gravel roads, long driveways, creative architecture, large vegetable gardens, a community hall and a general store that serves as the island's downtown are all endemic to island living.

DISTANCE	9.2 km/5.7 mi (2/3 gravel)
LEVEL	Easy to moderate
HIGHLIGHTS	Chickadee Lake; Pickles Road
START	Denman Island General Store

The Route

①   From the store, ride past the community hall on Northwest Road.

② (3.1 km / 1.9 mi)   At the stop sign, turn R onto Lake Road. (For the next 5 km [3.1 mi], the road surface is gravel.)

③ (4.5 km / 2.8 mi)   Having passed Chickadee Lake (seen through the trees and swimmable) on your L, turn R onto Central Road.

④ (6.3 km / 3.9 mi)   At a T-junction, turn R onto the unsigned Pickles Road.

⑤ (8.0 km / 5.0 mi)   Pickles Road ends at paved Denman Road (and its oversized public-notice board). Turn R onto Denman, descend the short but steep hill, and follow the road back to the store.

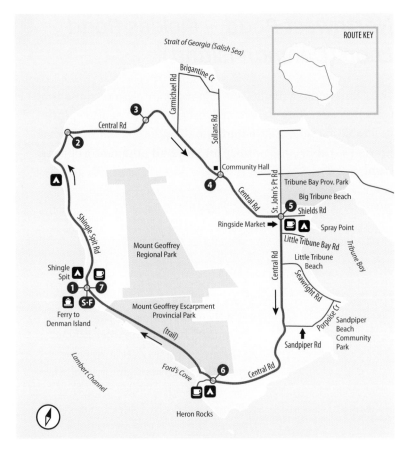

• *Waiting for the Denman Island ferry.*

South Hornby Island Loop

Hornby Island is known as a mountain biker's paradise. But for the more risk-averse among us, the island is also perfect for just plain old touring. This tour of the island's central and southern parts takes you to the celebrated Ringside Market, where you can eat delicious food and buy anything from books to jewellery to pottery and myriad other craft objects. Although the ride finishes opposite a pub, and despite what I wrote above about mountain biking, you have to negotiate 2 km (1.2 mi) of single-track hillside trail before you get there.

DISTANCE	17.8 km/11 mi
LEVEL	Moderate
HIGHLIGHTS	Community hall; Cardboard House Bakery; Ringside Market; Ford's Cove; Mount Geoffrey Escarpment Park Trail
START	Hornby Island ferry terminal at Shingle Spit

The Route

①   From the terminal, continue on Shingle Spit Road.

② (3.6 km / 2.2 mi)   At a sharp R turn, Shingle Spit Road becomes Central Road.

③ (5.6 km / 3.5 mi)   Hornby's famous Cardboard House Bakery is on your L.

④ (7.8 km / 4.8 mi)   On the L is the creatively designed and built island community hall. The island's library, medical centre and school are just around the corner.

⑤ (9.6 km / 6.0 mi)   At the junction of Central and St. John's Point roads is the Hornby Island Co-op and its Ringside Market.

Turn R here to follow Central Road as it heads for Ford's Cove, which has a marina, a government dock and a general store and café.

⑥ (14.3 km / 8.9 mi)   Just before the final descent into Ford's Cove, look for and take a wide trail on your R signed Mount Geoffrey Escarpment Park Trail to Shingle Spit. The trail soon narrows into a single track. Along the trail's length are two wooden bridges with stairs. (Walking is always an option!)

⑦ (17.8 km / 11.1 mi)   The trail ends opposite the Thatch Pub, close to the ferry terminal.

- **Above:** *Hornby Islanders' favourite bakery.*
- **Right:** *Hornby Island artistry.*

Helliwell Provincial Park's spectacular cliffs, Hornby Island.

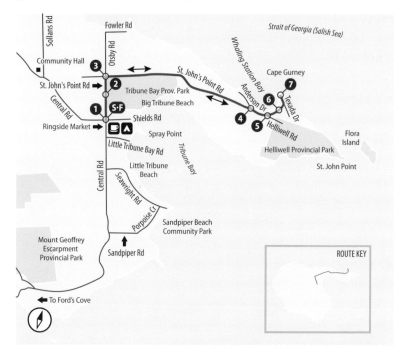

Sollans Rd
Fowler Rd
Otsby Rd
Strait of Georgia (Salish Sea)
Community Hall
3
Whaling Station Bay
Cape Gurney
St. John's Point Rd
2
St. John's Point Rd
7
Central Rd
Tribune Bay Prov. Park
Anderson Dr
6
Texada Dr
1
S·F
Big Tribune Beach
4
5
Ringside Market
Shields Rd
Helliwell Rd
Flora Island
Spray Point
Little Tribune Bay Rd
Tribune Bay
Helliwell Provincial Park
Central Rd
Little Tribune Beach
St. John Point
Seawright Rd
Porpoise Cr
Sandpiper Beach Community Park
Mount Geoffrey Escarpment Provincial Park
Sandpiper Rd

ROUTE KEY

◄ To Ford's Cove

ISLAND POTTERS

• *Ringside Market, Hornby Island.*

Ringside Market to Whaling Station Bay (Hornby Island)

This eastern part of Hornby has one of the most exquisite parcels of parkland in the entire archipelago: Helliwell Provincial Park, endowed with grassy headlands, clifftop trails, windblown Garry oaks, towering Douglas firs, cedars and expansive views over the Salish Sea. Also on this short ride, you'll get to visit two other Gulf Island gems – Tribune Bay Provincial Park and Whaling Station Bay; both have beaches that will tempt you off your bike.

DISTANCE	10.4 km / 6.5 mi (return)
LEVEL	Easy
HIGHLIGHTS	Tribune Bay Provincial Park; Helliwell Provincial Park; Whaling Station Bay; Ringside Market
START	Ringside Market

The Route

①   Leave the market from its large sign and ride north along St. John's Point Road.

② (0.5 km / 0.3 mi)   The entrance to Tribune Bay Provincial Park is on the R. This park is renowned for its sandy crescent beach.

③ (0.9 km / 0.6 mi)   Turn sharply R, keeping to St. John's Point Road. (Helliwell Provincial Park is signed at this corner.)

④ (4.0 km / 2.5 mi)   St. John's Point Road joins and becomes Anderson Drive.

⑤ (4.4 km / 2.7 mi)   On the R is the entrance road to Helliwell Provincial Park, 400 m (440 yd) away.

⑥ (4.9 km / 3.0 mi)   You are now at Whaling Station Bay. There are two beach accesses on your L before you turn L onto Texada Drive.

⑦ (5.2 km / 3.2 mi)   Road's end. Retrace your route to Ringside Market.

ACKNOWLEDGEMENTS

To my many friends who have joined me, over the years, in the pleasure of exploring the islands of the southern Salish Sea; to Frances Hunter for another of her thoughtful and creative book designs; to Amy Rutherford for her deceptively simple but elegant maps; to Don Gorman who believed in this project – to them all go my gratitude and appreciation.

JOHN CROUCH is a well-known athlete and writer who has published three successful guidebooks: *Bike Victoria* (2012), *Walk Victoria* (2009), and *Hike Victoria* (2008), along with a memoir, *Six Highways to Home: A Cycling Journey from Whitehorse to Victoria* (2014). For ten years he was the editor of a professional medical journal, the BC Massage Practitioner, and was founding editor of Island Runner magazine. John's physical and athletic pursuits embrace a number of disciplines. As a hiker and climber he has summited Mount Rainier, Mount Whitney, Mount Baker and Vancouver Island's highest peak, the Golden Hinde. As an athlete John has competed in well-over a dozen marathons and countless shorter races. He lives with his wife, Lorinda, in Victoria, British Columbia.